I0796720

Know Yourself

Published in 2026 by The School of Life
First published in the USA in 2026
930 High Road, London, N12 9RT

Authorised representative in the EEA:
The School of Life Amsterdam, Frederiksplein 54,
1017 XN Amsterdam, Netherlands

Designed and typeset by @marciamihotichstudio
Printed in Lithuania by Balto Print

A proportion of this book has appeared online at
www.theschooloflife.com/articles

The School of Life publishes a range of books on essential topics in psychological and emotional life, including relationships, parenting, friendship, careers and fulfilment. The aim is always to help us to understand ourselves better – and thereby to grow calmer, less confused and more purposeful. Discover our full range of titles, including books for children, here:
www.theschooloflife.com/books

The School of Life also offers a comprehensive therapy service, which complements, and draws upon, our published works:
www.theschooloflife.com/therapy

www.theschooloflife.com

ISBN 978-1-916753-45-7

10 9 8 7 6 5 4 3 2 1

Know Yourself

The School of Life

Contents

Introduction

One of the greater paradoxes of being human is that we must live within minds whose folds and depths we will never properly know. We, the most plausible experts on ourselves, are fated to go to our graves having made sense of only a slender portion of who we have been. Whole archives of sensations, thoughts, insights and intuitions will, in the end, dissolve away without record – the equivalent of the Great Library of Alexandria going up in flames every time a ventilator is switched off. We dwell in a mansion made up of corridors, vaults and rooms, only a few of which we will be able to explore in the time that remains. We are armed with feeble torches with which to try to make sense of a vast darkness within us.

Occasionally, we pick up hints of how much might be at play in our minds. We wake up from a dream in which worlds and people we had no sense of knowing emerge with disorienting immediacy. Or, while tossing fitfully in bed on a humid night, we collide with slices of our lives we had lost any active memory of: the dawn light over the sea, a pair of gloves from early childhood, the light in the hallway when we took an ex-partner home for the first time two decades ago, the seat of a taxi as we made our way across town on an autumn afternoon. None of it, perhaps, ever disappears. Unexpected bits of us constantly surge up unbidden from certain sorts of biscuits, textures of carpet, smells and evening and morning light.

Our minds have been encoded over long years of which we have no concrete recollection. Just as we speak a language without any memory of its acquisition, so too the emotional forces that shaped our personalities grow invisible to us, leaving their imprint but not their cast. The grounds for most of our responses lie outside our understanding.

If we were to pause and undertake the curious exercise of asking ourselves – with particular intent – what we were really feeling at a given moment, we might become conscious of an implausibly broad and simultaneous array of concerns and feelings. We might, for example, have a concurrent sense that we have an appointment at midday, that there is a slight scab on our right hand, that we're under the pall of a tetchy exchange that took place several hours earlier with our partner, that the words of a maddening song are playing over and over in our mind ('*Because only you belong ... ahhah ... because only you belong ... ahhah*'), that we're starting to comprehend an anxiety around a meeting tomorrow, that we miss M and the playfulness of the other night, that the arch of our foot aches uncomfortably, that we've been left guilty by an article in the paper, that there's someone bouncing a ball outside, that the colour of the vitamin packet on the desk is exactly that of the cupboard in our classroom in primary school, that a colleague was strangely abrupt with us on Friday, that we have to collect a pair of trousers from the dry cleaner's after we've had lunch, that there is a strange-sounding bird squawking outside, that we'd like to stretch our back, that there is something almost religious waiting to emerge inside us ... And this, of course, is only a ridiculously curtailed summary of what might really be going on at any specific point. Rather than attempting to describe it in linear prose, it might be better to resort to a gigantic map of the kind they use to represent the stars, in which all the elements of consciousness might be pictured like so many galaxies and constellations, some near, others many light years away, in the boundless sky of the inner mind.

Partly, we're encouraged to miss some of our own intricacy because we take our cue from other people and they, from the outside, appear so much simpler than they are. The human face is a misleading organ that doesn't let on about the hesitancy, richness, confusion, genius, muddle and obscurity within. The eyes don't hint at the torrent of images we see whenever we close them; the mouth doesn't reveal the internal polyphonic murmur we hear whenever we are in silence. In company, people speak in more or less meaningful sentences; they lift from their streams of consciousness a few relatively upbeat and comprehensible phrases. In response to a question as to how they are, they'll say, 'Oh not too bad, all things considered ...' They'll let us know that they had 'a quiet weekend' or are 'going to take a few days off to see Mum.' And we start to forget what brutal summaries these are. We don't accord to other people the knowledge we have from inside ourselves, namely that we contain worlds. Novelists further rush over the subtleties, and help us to forget who we are, by writing sentences like 'Amanda decided she needed to end her relationship' or 'Abdul realised he was after a change of career' – as though any real human has ever *thought* in such clear-cut and purposive ways.

The difficulty we have in understanding ourselves is not merely an intellectual puzzle; it's what ends up powering our greatest psychic pains. It's because we have such trouble working out what we feel, who we are, what we want and what is motivating us that we end up marrying the wrong people, pursuing unfulfilling careers, failing to connect properly with friends, spending our money inappropriately, squabbling with innocent colleagues and passing on a raft of our problems to the next generation. We become beset by foreboding that we can't trace back to anything concrete. Or we feel hemmed in, unfree and burdened by a weight of unthought thoughts, uninterpreted emotions and unfelt feelings. It's because of our self-ignorance that we can't determine whether we're feeling love or obsession, that we can't work out the origins of our anxieties and that we surprise ourselves with the extent of our irritability or rage when we lose our sunglasses or discover the Sellotape isn't where we expected it to be.

The mind tries to give us signs when we are failing to understand it as well as it requires. It sends us headaches to stir our conscience; it emits twitches and neurotic compulsions; we find we can't sleep or we develop addictions to exercise, drugs or the news. We suffer the mind's desperate and creative revenge for all the thoughts we have refused to entertain.

If we are fortunate, we can find encouragement to interrupt our mania; we may pause, take a week off, travel somewhere remote – and start the arduous business of looking inside. We can wonder why things are not as straightforward as we had imagined: why our relationships keep failing, why our back is so tight, why sleep never comes and why we are so scared of disaster.

When Socrates, apparently the wisest man of antiquity, was asked to define our highest purpose as humans, he offered a still-legendary answer: 'To know ourselves.' Without self-knowledge, all other efforts will be in vain. It won't matter how much money we have or what achievements we have attained or how many friends we can lay claim to, there will be unexplained despair and nightmares.

That the task of self-knowledge is fated to remain incomplete is no argument against it; it is the dedication that counts. We should aspire to be people who never cease to try to make sense of themselves, who want to be able to understand how their childhoods have shaped them, to know what their attachment style is or where reality ends and their projections begin. It's a mark of maturity not to be offended or thrown off course by someone who asks us for more information on how we might be complicated or 'a bit mad', given that we all are, and to know that the closest any of us ever come to sanity is through intuiting some of the ways in which we might be unwell. We should devote ourselves to constantly trying to shrink the scale of the darkness within us, bringing what was once in shadow closer to the light of interpretation, so that we stand a chance of being slightly less frantic, intemperate and unpredictable to others and ourselves.

The prerequisites for the task of self-knowledge are patience, guile and limitless humility. We'll need to call on some of the remorselessness of an angler and the persistence of a lepidopterist. We'll need to catch ourselves unawares: we'll need to be curious in the early hours after waking up from a dream, or in twilight moods of tiredness when our defences are low and our true yearnings can be felt twitching in the background, or on long quiet evenings when we can sift through thoughts and ideas without censorship or concern for being normal. If we are fortunate and devoted, gradually, we may start to lay claim to certain insights. Sections of the map can be filled in; we'll have a sense of what our childhoods did to us, what exaggerated fears and behaviours we may be carrying, what unhelpful things we do when people love us (and when they don't), why we fall into moods at specific times of the day. There may – thanks to long years of work – be a more reliable connection between what we consciously register and what is really happening in us. We'll know where a mood of persecution is coming from; we'll be able to trace a link between the unfriendly conversation yesterday and the feeling of shame today. The quality of our detective work will rise. We may shorten the distance between feeling and expression, understand a little more of what we want and what we might be suited to, piece together why we are tricky around certain people who appear to remind us of characters from our pasts, comprehend the games we are trying to invite people to play with us who don't deserve or want them, recognise the history of moods and tendencies that hold us back and discern why we might be compelled to fail or hurt ourselves. We will –

with greater self-knowledge – be better able to apologise where appropriate, to be less in need of defensive strategies, to be able to admit to more and to deny less, to be more stable and funnier because we'll have a better hold on our contradictions and the gulf between who we hope to be and who we are.

Modern society gives us no shortage of ambitions. We will have landed on the option with the best chance of bringing us peace and freedom when we can dare to begin the inward journey.

I.

Selfhood

The burden of childhood

One of the more distinctive, and at the same time irritating – even maddening – habits of the modern world is its repeated suggestion that the explanation for who we are must, in the end, always come down to what happened to us in our childhoods.

No other age, besides our own, has thought in this pre-determined way. No ancient Egyptian or Sumerian or Inca ever entertained such a prescriptive notion – which they would probably have considered as peculiar as we do their beliefs in the sun god Ra or the fertility goddess Pachamama. No mediaeval knight or Phoenician trader likely paused their activities to mull over a slight at the hands of a mother or father when they were 5, and no premodern monarch or poet is on record supposing that their adult challenges might have been the result of incidents of disapproval or neglect in the nursery.

It's not hard to see why we might inwardly bristle at our modern story of childhood as the source of all of our identities. How insulting to our many adult achievements to have to believe that our characters might have been decisively moulded by a past we can barely remember – and whose impact cannot easily be altered. How disheartening to hear that the course of seven or eight decades of adult life should be masterminded by events that predated our acquisition of reason or speech – and that to stand any chance of shifting the early legacy, we might need to go back and explore it in exhaustive detail over many years. A childhood focus seems to strip us of agency, hope or will.

It asks us to look with suspicion at the behaviour of people who may be ailing or departed and who probably did their best, all things considered. Families are seldom in the mood for an in-depth audit of their emotional functioning. It is natural that we might prefer to lean on the evidence of photo albums with their record of boisterous birthday parties, picnics and foreign holidays – as opposed to those darker times when everyone may have been sulking in their rooms or shouting, and no one felt like picking up a camera.

Our vulnerability to childhood events has been as hard to learn to see as our exposure to aspects of microbial life. It took until late in the 19th century for humanity to take on board the extraordinary suggestion that a whole city might be poisoned by a wholly invisible bacterial element that might be lurking in an ostensibly clear jug of water – just as it has taken us a similar number of centuries to appreciate that a whole life might be thrown off course by a belittling approach from a parent, or a few moments of inappropriate touching by a caregiver. It remains both appalling and surprising that so-called 'small things' could have such power to destroy us.

For most of history, we were shielded from recognising the impact of childhood by the sheer harshness of existence. We could – most of us – expect to be dead by 30. Survival was the priority, not flourishing or happiness. There wasn't much energy left – in the unending struggle – to notice that the fishmonger's wife could not trust anyone, that the cobbler's son was anxious around authority or that the downcast knight might be incapable of intimacy. We lacked the strength, calmness and patience to work out the elusive dynamics that were tearing us apart. It was only once life had found a degree of stability, once there was running water, enough to eat and lighting along well-policed streets, that we could start to look up from our immediate perils. And in a new district of Vienna outside the old city walls, an especially thorough and determined middle-class Jewish doctor proposed new theories through which we could learn to appreciate some of the less obvious origins of the screams inside us.

Now that we know, our particular responsibility is not to forget, but to keep in mind the vulnerable truths that have been uncovered. We have to have the courage to incorporate our true susceptibility into our picture of ourselves. It may well be the case that we have been thrown off course by shortfalls of care and affection; it may just be that our anxiety or despair have their roots in early neglect. If we have to suffer, we should not – to compound our miseries – pretend that we are simpler than we are. We should make a graceful accommodation with our emotional knottedness and take all necessary measures to address it. We should gird ourselves for our fussiness and our fragility. We shouldn't be shocked if we need to divert an unholy degree of time to unpicking the early years. Our difficulties are par for the course; they are what we should expect to befall the most complicated and sensitive animal in the universe.

Our true needs

Because children are brought up in so many different ways, and because we have natural tendencies not to want to pass judgement or sound moralistic, we are collectively apt to miss the extent to which we can hazard some generalisations about what any child will need emotionally in order to flourish. We should not continue to imagine that it is simply luck that one person ends up mired in distress and terror in adulthood and another feels free and creative, that one person is able to form good relationships and another can't, that one person feels at peace with themselves and another despises their own being. There are causes in the past and – frighteningly, for anyone involved in the genesis and care of children – commensurate burdens of responsibility.

We might summarise some of the requirements for a viable start as follows:

- First and foremost, a child depends on feeling powerfully wanted. It seems we cannot matter to ourselves without first having mattered very much to another. To have the courage to stay on our own side through the vicissitudes of life, we rely on a sure early impression that our existence was of boundless concern to a few people close to us. Someone needs to have thought the day of our arrival was as close to the happiest of their life, someone needs to have lit up when we walked in the room, someone needs to have sympathised with us when we had a paper cut or a nightmare.

- If a child is to grow up into someone without a constant need for praise and worship, they must – for a limited but crucial period in babyhood – be able to feel like minor royalty. They need to get milk when they want it, they shouldn't be left to cry 'to teach them a lesson', they shouldn't permanently be suspected of growing 'spoilt' (when they are 6 months old). Narcissists and the grandiose aren't those who have basked for too long in the admiration of others; they are those who need to puff themselves up because they never had their necessary fill of attention. No one ever grew ill from too much tenderness.

- In a fortunate start, there aren't excessive demands for compliance. The child doesn't need to be a 'good' boy or girl all the time; they don't need to lie and smile to win affection or appease an angry or depressed caregiver. They don't, out of fear, need to ingratiate themselves and follow the party line at any cost. They can be unusual, and their more complicated emotions honoured. They can be sad on holiday. They don't have to love Granny. Maybe school isn't brilliant. They can be jealous of their younger sibling. Their reality doesn't have to be sacrificed on an altar of propriety.

- The fortunate child has caregivers whose own needs for glory, attention and praise have been appeased elsewhere. They can bear to put their own longings for acclaim aside for the sake of another. There is a lot these caregivers don't feel compelled to reveal. They can edit and restrain themselves into calmer, more digestible, slightly fictionalised versions of themselves called 'mother' or 'father'.

- The good-enough parent strives to look at matters through the child's distinctive point of view. They get down on their knees when they speak to them; they try to imagine what it would be like to worry intensely about nounou-rabbit's tail dropping off or that a page in a favourite story book had inadvertently been torn or that a door had slammed slightly precipitously. They can attune themselves to a new, foreign frequency.

- The good-enough parent can remember their own dependence and vulnerability without horror. They have a settled relationship with their own original incompetence and naivety. They don't, therefore, need to guard against memories of their weakness through exaggerated displays of strength or cynicism. They have confidence that their child will grow out of their elemental states soon enough – and will do so all the better if they are not roughly told to grow up.

- The good-enough parent isn't so proud or attached to their own dignity that they won't sometimes be able to get on the floor and pretend to be a donkey or a dromedary.

- The good-enough parent doesn't rely on the child's approval so much that they cannot say 'no' when the occasion demands it – and send the young charge to bed immediately now that it's late and there is school tomorrow. They will stay steady (and even smile inside) when they are solemnly told that they are going to be loathed 'until eternity' for not giving way. They will calmly appreciate that they need sometimes to be hated – in the name of allowing a child the privilege of feeling that its desires are limited and its powers circumscribed. They understand how scary it is to be allowed to do whatever one wishes.

- The good-enough parent doesn't need the child to shine in the areas of their own insecurities. Perhaps the child can be very bad at maths and dislike reading. Perhaps they can have few friends and make no impact on the school authorities. They are granted the luxury to define success and failure by themselves.

- The fortunate child's caregivers have from the outset made their peace with eventually being outgrown. They don't need to make the child ill so that they can always have a role or instil guilt so that there can be visits every weekend. They know that they will have succeeded when they are no longer constantly in demand. They are – almost – content to be forgotten.

This is some of what we all need to have a chance to grow up feeling free and unfrightened. These are the markers of what we can term a properly privileged childhood. This can be the start of a map of what might be missing.

The impacts of childhood

Whenever we see a struggling adult, someone who cannot bear to be loved or who is cross all the time, has no courage to be themselves or needs to be continually proved right, without necessarily understanding much of their story, we can hazard a guess: somewhere long ago, there was a shortfall of love. Love stands in relation to the demands of the growing emotional mind as vitamins stand to those of the developing body. Whenever there is mental unwellness, we can know that there will have been a failure of care and attunement, that there will have been an absence of tolerance and sympathy, that there will have been a failure to honour a small person's reality.

Some of the following emotional laws are in operation:

- If someone is early on denied a sense that they matter, they will struggle all their lives to feel sufficiently significant to others. They may adopt a retiring manner or put on exaggerated displays of status or take to the stage and try to win themselves an audience, but the wound will be similar: they will be saddled with an ongoing sense that they do not deserve to be here. We cannot bear our own selves if we were not once very solidly at the centre of another's world.

- If someone could not count on a primary caregiver who was warm and dependable, cosy and focused, they will doubt every candidate for love who later presents themselves for their consideration. Without knowing what is happening, they will trust no one; they will declare every potential partner to be boring, unattractive or 'weird' (for thinking better of them than they think of themselves). They may be charming on a date, they may long for a family, but they will be mercilessly drawn to destroy every relationship that is at risk of working.

- If someone didn't model for us how to communicate our real intentions, if someone didn't give us an example of how to speak our needs, we will be angry but not realise it, we will sulk yet pretend we don't care, we will say we're fine when we're crying inside; we'll have no confidence that a conversation can ever work.

- If we were furious but were told to be good, if we were angry but weren't allowed to bother anyone, if we desperately had to appease someone to hang on to the love we depended on, we'll be malleable conformists who know how to adjust ourselves perfectly to all prevailing expectations ... other than our own.

- If we were terrified – if there was constant shouting or a feeling of foreboding – the world won't ever feel stable. Anxiety will be a constant. Sleep will be hard to find. The catastrophe that once occurred will be continually projected forward; something will always be anticipated to be on the verge of going very wrong – again.

- If our body was not cared for, if our boundaries were not respected or our appearance was not cherished, it will be hard not to despise the way we look; it will be hard to contemplate ourselves in the mirror, to sleep comfortably in the same room as someone else, to exercise as regularly as we want to, to eat in a way that is kind to ourselves. The heart may well get exhausted early; it will be difficult not to pick at our skin. Our body will know the score.

- If we were told we were a genius from the get-go, if we were assured we would have a golden destiny but had no idea how or why, if someone needed us to be special to compensate them for their own sense of ordinariness, we'll struggle all our lives to accept what is humdrum and routine in ourselves. We won't ever taste the luxury of being allowed simply to exist.

- If we were never listened to, making space for another will feel too much of a burden. How can we learn to attend to someone else's complexity when, at the crucial early period, no one bothered to give our own distinctive existence the attention it needed?

- If we learnt that the only way to be noticed was to make a drama or act seductively or to be extremely and inauthentically good, or very bad, how do we dare to kick such habits (let alone even become aware of them) in later years when they have ceased to have anything to do with our own interests?

We are – most of us – experts in spotting and complaining about why other people are difficult. We should, when we feel strong enough, have the courage to understand and accept why – which ultimately requires us to take on board the full, lamentable reality that the world is mad and off-kilter not because of politics or technology or finance but because we don't first and foremost, at a collective level, begin to know how to love and care for small people.

What happened to me?

Even if we accept the theory that adults can be decisively shaped by what happened to them early on, we may not be able to see how this objectively plausible concept applies to us at a granular level. We don't – most of us – have any ready ability to work out exactly what might have happened in our particular pasts to make us the unusual, unhappy or difficult people we often are today.

One way to conceive of events is to understand that we learnt a language of emotional behaviours – and did so in a process analogous to that of more standard language acquisition. It's one of the miracles of nature that a child will, between the ages of 0 and 5, unconsciously and without making any fuss, master pretty much every rule of syntax of whatever language happens to be spoken around them. While they're putting their teddies to bed, figuring out how buttons work or drawing buttercups, they are quietly becoming expert grammarians and expanding their inner dictionaries with around ten new words a day.

Something similar is going on at the emotional level. Here too, without anyone paying attention, a child is scanning the immediate environment and taking in its prevailing 'grammar': what happens when you try to get someone's attention? What does the man in the vicinity do when he is challenged? How responsive is that woman to our needs? How reliable are people?

We also know – from the linguistic example – how hard it will be to shift our mental map once it has been established. Those unfortunate middle-aged students trying painstakingly to learn Spanish or Korean are telling us something about how fixed patterns can get. Someone who associates relationships with fear or who believes that the route to attention lies in rebellion can be expected to have as much of a challenge reconfiguring their expectations as does a 43-year-old who sets out to become fluent in Finnish or Mandarin.

There is an added complication. When it comes to standard language, we know roughly what tongue we are speaking in: we can say that we're English speakers or fluent in French. But when it comes to emotional language, we are akin to under-travelled people who lack any sense that they are even conversing in a particular dialect; expressing ourselves as we do seems the natural and invisible option.

It can take a long time before we realise that our dialect is in fact supremely regional, specific to the particular locale and household we were formed in, that, in fact, not everyone trembles when a particular tone is used, that not everyone feels it's normal never to speak up, that some people more readily trust and have no inhibitions around joy, that not all men or women are as we experienced our caregivers.

To change our language, we have to notice what we have taken entirely for granted. We might start by asking ourselves some large questions to sharpen our impression of distinctiveness:

- In love, how much are we able to trust that someone will be kind and good?
- In sex, can we feel accepted and at ease?
- Do we feel at home in our bodies?
- What do we do when someone doesn't understand us?
- How much confidence do we have that our voice can be heard?

- To what extent do we feel – in ourselves – like good-enough people?
- How much faith do we have that others will hear us when we speak?

We can know, in general terms, that every negative or tricky answer relates to a challenge in the past. We may not know more at this stage, but we can know that we have a history, that something was learnt – and that knowledge of what this was might in time set us free.

We can catch more of what is inside our minds by learning to spot how we generalise. We can ask ourselves to complete certain sentences without thinking for too long, in order to encourage our spontaneous background assumptions to surge forward:

- *Men in general are …*
- *Women in general are …*
- *If I am happy …*
- *If someone knew me …*
- *My body …*
- *I am …*
- *People are …*
- *In the end …*

We can, similarly, look at pictures where we can't know too much of what is actually going on – for example, of a mother and child or two lovers or a father and his daughter – and explore our intuitive sense of what might be at stake: who loves who? What is everyone feeling? What might happen next? The key is that we can't know exactly, but we can have a strong sense nevertheless, and that sense is likely to be telling us a lot more about ourselves than it does about reality. Our responses hold clues to the way we characteristically steer ourselves through the world, waiting for particular things to happen at the hands of others – because of certain specific things that once happened to us, from which we are generalising outwards without much awareness that we are doing so. From this, we may be committing a grave injustice against those around us. They may not be angry with us at all – but we are sure they are because someone once was. They may be eminently worthy of our trust; we just don't think so because someone else of their gender might not have been.

We are – each one of us – looking out at the world, in some direction or another, through heavily distorted lenses formed by a past that we cannot easily perceive. We begin the journey towards self-knowledge when we can accept the extent to which we have, for so long, had no clue how distinctive our perspective has been, how much of our past we have taken for granted, how little of our native language we have noticed.

Owen Harvey, *Ryan, Sid and Freya*, 2019

What will happen to them? What does the older girl feel? What does the baby feel? What are the father's intentions and thoughts? What we find in the picture belongs as much to our own pasts and situations as it does to anything in the image itself.

The basic realisations

Self-awareness might be said to involve a set of fundamental realisations about the relationship between past and present.

1. Who I am today is, to a humbling and maddening degree, the result of events and dynamics from a lengthy childhood I cannot for the most part remember, almost certainly don't seek to explore and am understandably invested in trying to think well of.

2. Most of our difficulties come down to a shortfall in love and attunement in childhood. The physical vulnerability of children has its counterpart in an elevated degree of emotional susceptibility. Not very much needs to have happened in order for us to pick up a substantial wound.

3. We spend a great deal of energy trying not to understand our pasts in the name of maintaining our poise, our illusions and our self-respect. Most of who we are lies in the unconscious.

4. What we feel will happen next around people in general carries complex echoes of what happened back then around certain people in particular. With great

unfairness, we constantly attribute to people in the here and now motives and likely patterns of behaviour unknowingly derived from figures from our histories.

5. We become slightly less difficult to be around when we start to appreciate the extent to which we are continually distorting reality through lenses scratched by our pasts. Maturity means no longer insisting too hard on our sanity.

6. To go back over the past – the work of personal archaeology – is almost certainly going to be a mixture of frightening and irritating. It would be extremely odd if we didn't have very mixed feelings about the entire business of self-examination.

Mechanisms of defence

Getting to know ourselves better sounds, on the surface, like a project we might all buy into. But this is to underestimate the extent to which we are, just below the surface, typically highly invested in *not* getting to know or feel a range of important but troubling things about who we are. Whatever lip service we may pay to the project of self-knowledge, we would – it seems – very much like *not* to know a great deal about our identities.

In order to shield us from ourselves, we rely on techniques known as mechanisms of defence: a range of astonishingly clever internal manoeuvres that subtly enable us to expel uncomfortable ideas from our awareness without alerting our conscience and so return us to a blind, placid equilibrium. It is thanks to our mechanisms of defence that we're able to convince ourselves we hate someone we're actually drawn to (but can't have) or that we get depressed in lieu of getting angry with a person who has done us wrong but who we want to believe is good.

However effective they may be, mechanisms of defence ultimately impose a great psychic cost on us; they tie up our energies, repressing ideas on which our growth relies. They mire us in symptoms and secondary illnesses. Every denied thought creates a drag on our minds; every unfelt feeling generates an underground whirlpool of repressed energy. Our defences buy us short-term calm at the expense of long-term development.

Developing an understanding of the way mechanisms of defence work won't magically save us from reliance on them, but it may give us an inkling of what we are up to and increase our tolerance to insight.

None of us are without defences. What we call a person's character is, in large measure, the result of the particular set of defence mechanisms they rely on; it's the outcome of the distinctive ways in which they have opted to defend themselves against the painful sides of their reality.

A list of our mechanisms of defence might include the following:

The grandiose defence

Once upon a time, we felt catastrophically insignificant; once we were humiliated and ignored by our caregivers and denied a basic sense that we had a right to exist. Many years later, grown and more capable, with arch rigidity, we make use of money, reputation and cultural capital to insist on a specialness that we can't – for that matter – ever truly believe in. We wield grandiosity as a shield against the risks of any renewed encounter with the neglected, powerless, desperate child still sobbing and forlorn somewhere inside us.

The common-sense defence

We are filled with huge and painfully complicated truths; they might be about sexuality, love or money. There is so much that we might need to think about and would, as a result, need to mourn or grapple anxiously with. But we lack the courage and the wherewithal and therefore settle on a highly consoling line of defence: that the whole field of psychology, the discipline that tries to draw our attention to ourselves, is so much hype and 'psychobabble'. We dismiss its efforts as specious nonsense; we pride ourselves on calling a spade a spade and cling fervently to the solacing thought that our minds are lacking any of the waywardness, complexity or folly that seems the universal lot.

The manic defence

We run strenuously from one project to another; we give ourselves no time at all to sit with our odder wishes and fears. It might have been a year since we last had a day without commitments. We devote manic energy to something, anything – work, the news, exercise, literature, drugs, gardening – to keep our unresolved thoughts at bay. The most terrifying prospect in the world might be to sit in a silent room with ourselves.

The sadistic defence

We choose to feel strong and in control by subjecting another to the pains we once endured as children. We make a junior colleague feel inept, we ensure our offspring knows how little they are worth, we criticise our partner for their countless departures from perfection. There are, in our deep minds, only two roles a person can play: victim or perpetrator. And we have firmly decided the one we'd rather be.

The masochistic defence

We feel too weak to prevent ourselves from suffering, but not too weak to turn our suffering into a sort of choice, even – in a manner of speaking – a kind of pleasure. So we go in active search of partners who won't fulfil us, we make very sure we criticise ourselves in the wake of every success, we gain a particular relish in being treated badly once again. We know we are going to suffer; but at least – this time around – we are in charge of inflicting the pain on ourselves.

The avoidant defence

We might like so much to be close to others. But as certain people hurt us intolerably when we originally tried to be so, we have come to an easier and more bearable position: we don't in fact need anyone at all. Talk of emotional connection is exaggerated. We very much enjoy sport or needlework and would – sincerely – far prefer to spend the weekend, or the rest of our lives, in our own company.

The early-retirement defence

There is much that is – troublingly – rather great about us. We are clever, we can be charming, we might triumph socially or professionally. But such victories carry enormous risks. Someone we once relied on for survival was not comfortable with success; someone preferred it if we messed up. And so we fail repeatedly out of subterranean loyalty to a threatening and threatened caregiver. Internally hemmed in by an invisible choice between victory and abandonment, we retire early from the perils of victory. People wonder why we gave up some pursuit or another. 'They showed so much promise ...' they muse, and that – of course – was precisely the problem.

The self-hatred defence

Someone was once very unkind to us; someone once left us feeling frightened and insignificant. We should – in all fairness – hate them back in equal measure but that would be too wounding to our innate modesty and our wish to think well of those in whose care we began. So, we rely on an alternative fiction: that our caregivers were fine enough, the problem lay with us. We were not treated abysmally; we happen to be awful. Harm wasn't done to us; we are entirely stupid or ugly. We don't live in a world of random injustice; we deserved the ill-treatment we received. We deem our problems deserved rather than encounter a greatly more troubling thought: someone we adored was very cruel to us.

The magical defence

The laws of science can be appallingly harsh; the laboratory results mean that we are going to develop a chronic disease within a few years. The laws of economic and romantic probability can be as arduous; we may now never come into great wealth or meet an ideal partner. And precisely because the truth is so vile, we think with the basic premises of reality. If we eat the root of a certain plant, adopt a particular conspiracy theory, chant a certain mantra or visualise health or success hard enough, we will defeat the 'rational' naysayers. Magical thinking turns despair into delusion.

The cynical defence

There can be protection in cynicism too. We resort to cynicism to avoid the torment of our own expectations. It becomes easier to believe we are doomed, that life is inherently awful and that satisfaction is always a mirage – rather than risk the further torments of promise.

Weaning ourselves from reliance on these mechanisms of defence is the work of a lifetime. We don't easily let go of techniques that are so effective at sparing us pain. To surrender these mechanisms requires a leap of faith: that the price will eventually be worth it, that our symptoms will abate the more we understand them, that we will live more easily once we nurture the roots of self-awareness. A true adult – that ever-elusive goal – might be defined as someone with a no-longer-so-powerful need to deny: someone willing at last to pay the real price for knowing their truth.

The unconscious

One of the great discoveries of the 20th century was the region of the mind now universally referred to as *the unconscious*. According to this theory, only a part of our thoughts unfold in the full glare of conscious awareness, while a far larger and far more significant share do so under the cover of internal darkness.

Crucially, what relegates thoughts to the unconscious is their degree of emotional inadmissibility. We cannot think certain thoughts through properly because they pose such a challenge to our peace of mind and violate our self-image; they shatter illusions, they threaten to strip us of our pride. We simply cannot accept that we might – for example – have a different sexuality to what we had assumed, or that we might be much more cruel or angry or kind or hurt.

We end up chronically divided as a result: angry but unaware that we are so, desirous but cut off from the fact, afraid but unsure of what there is to fear, or why. And in this lack of awareness lie most of the sources of our unhappiness, our compulsions, our anger, our low moods and our counterproductive behaviours.

The goal of psychological life is, therefore, to try to turn as much of what was once unconscious into consciousness: to admit to as much as possible and to cease using up valuable energy warding off reality. We may never be able to empty the unconscious entirely but the more we can drain it of its evasiveness, the less nervous and inwardly compromised we will feel.

A person who has set to work on their unconscious might – with grace, sadness and humour – be able to admit to a range of things that they might formerly have protested angrily about. As self-examined people, we might be able to dwell comfortably alongside a range of unusual, hitherto taboo possibilities:

- Perhaps we are, after all, really very strange.
- Perhaps we are – very often – really quite stupid.

- Perhaps our sexuality isn't what we've made it out to be all along.

- Perhaps our feelings towards our parents are a lot more complicated than would be convenient.

- Perhaps we're not quite as kind, forgiving and tolerant as we are used to implying. Maybe we do want to triumph over, and crush, certain people. Maybe we aren't simply just 'nice'.

- Maybe we aren't as meek and modest as we're meant to be; maybe we can be greedy, aggressive and extremely competitive.

- Maybe we've been terribly unfair to many people. Perhaps it isn't always someone else's fault.

- Maybe we aren't remotely 'normal'; maybe we are in large part really rather perverted, weird, lost, sad and at sea. And that could – nevertheless – be very much OK.

All these thoughts, and more, lie on the other side of our internal defences and wait to be explored sanguinely once we've taken the decision to try to understand who we actually are.

The will to truth

It can seem from certain angles as if most of our psychic energy is devoted to repressing important truths about us, as if we are natural experts at denial and self-ignorance.

But that would be to miss another equally important part of our make-up: the part of us that – despite all the pain that might result and the discomfort involved – is in fact profoundly geared towards self-illumination; a part that desperately wants to know who we are, that is restlessly driven to unearth uncomfortable secrets, that wants everything in the open, that seeks to know as much of its nature as it can before it is too late – that lives under the sway of a momentous will to truth.

A way to read many so-called mental illnesses is as reflections of ongoing battles between the forces of repression and the forces of the will to truth. Our compulsions, our despair, our anxiety, our mood swings and our bodily pains represent a series of compromise positions between an aspiration to know ourselves and a strong wish not to.

The art of healing from these symptoms is to read them as – almost always – containing a denied part of our identity and as capable of being lessened the moment the puzzles become known.

When we cannot sleep, for example, it is frequently because there is something important that one part of the mind is trying to tell another but cannot. The sleeplessness is a desperate act on the part of our emotional conscience – urgently trying to alert us to ideas that we are refusing to take in during the day. We will have a chance to sleep once we develop a greater courage to know.

Similarly, we may fall into what we call depression when a side of us experiences an inadmissible degree of rage towards someone we are meant to love; it might be a spouse, a parent or a child. But once we allow our complexity to come through and give ourselves licence for a burst of legitimate frustration, our spirits may lift. Our mind won't need to be sad about everything because we have identified one or two particular people we needed – for a time at least – to be extremely annoyed with.

When we are truly closed to ourselves, our minds may feel they have no other option but to set off a bodily symptom. They will make our back ache intolerably. They will make our stomachs feel mysterious painful spasms. They will send our hearts racing. None of this is very pleasant but the will to truth may have grown desperate; there might be other ways to alert our sluggish intelligence than to tug at our sleeve through an illness.

We will get better the more we can allow ourselves to know our minds directly. Our will to truth is an unyielding partner and formidable opponent of our unconscious desires for ignorance. The more we can know who we are, the fewer symptoms we will need to endure.

The role of crises and breakdowns

It might seem as if the journey towards self-knowledge could proceed in a relatively smooth and linear way. But the battle between the forces of repression and the drive towards self-awareness tends to be far more bitter and entrenched than that. For years, there can be a stalemate, neither side yielding ground until the pressure to know grows intolerable and bursts forth in a spectacular explosion, like a trapped subterranean gas. Insofar as we learn about ourselves, it seems that we tend to do so in dramatic crises and breakdowns rather than (as would be more convenient) peaceful small daily epiphanies.

For a long time, we pretend to ourselves and others that all is well. We twitch occasionally, sometimes we are a lot more irritable than seems right, but we keep busy and wave away concerns. We keep showing up and being a good boy or girl, the way we've been trained to do.

Until, suddenly, one day, much to everyone's surprise, including our own, we might break. The rupture can take many forms. We can no longer get out of bed. We fall into a catatonic despair. We develop all-consuming social anxiety. We refuse to eat. We babble incoherently. We lose command over part of our body. We are compelled to do something scandalous, contrary to our normal selves. We become wholly paranoid in a given area. We refuse to play by the usual rules in our relationship; we have an affair, ramp up the fighting – or otherwise poke a very large stick in the wheels of day-to-day life.

The breakdown looks like madness, but it doesn't have to be random or senseless. It may be a bid for self-understanding, an attempt by one part of our minds to force the other into a process of growth, self-understanding and self-development which it has hitherto refused to undertake. If we can put it paradoxically, it may be an attempt to jumpstart a process of getting well, properly well, through a stage of falling very ill.

The danger, therefore, if we merely medicalise a breakdown and attempt to shift it away at once is that we will miss the lesson embedded within our sicknesses. A breakdown isn't just a pain, though it is that too, of course; it is a particular opportunity to learn.

The reason we *break* down is that we have not, over years, *flexed* very much. There were things we needed to hear inside our minds that we deftly put to one side; there were messages we needed to heed, bits of emotional learning and communicating we didn't do – and now, after being patient for so long, far too long, the emotional self is attempting to make itself heard in the only way it now knows how. It has become entirely desperate – and we should understand and even sympathise with its mute rage.

What the breakdown is telling us above anything else is that it must no longer be business as usual – that things have to change or (and this can be properly frightening to witness) that death might be preferable.

Why can't we simply listen to the emotional need calmly and in good time – and avoid the melodrama of a breakdown? Because the conscious mind is inherently lazy and squeamish and therefore reluctant to engage with what the breakdown eventually has to tell it with brutality.

A crisis represents an appetite for growth that hasn't until now found another way of expressing itself. After a horrific few months or years of breakdown, many people will say, 'I don't know how I'd ever have got well if I hadn't fallen ill.'

In the midst of a breakdown, we often wonder whether we have gone mad. We're behaving oddly, no doubt, but beneath the surface agitation, we are on a hidden yet logical search for health. We haven't become ill; we were ill already. Our crisis, if we can get through it, comprises an attempt to dislodge us from a toxic status quo and an insistent call to rebuild our lives on a more authentic and sincere basis.

Mental illness

The term 'mental illness' has a way of sounding so alien, cold and severe that it may – despite our best intentions – leave us struggling to understand what could be really going on for sufferers (who might at times include us).

A useful way to think of the term is to imagine that it involves a form of negative thinking that would be familiar to most people but which is here distinctive principally because of its relentlessness and restrictiveness. Like all of us, mentally unwell people feel anxiety; like all of us, they know self-hatred, paranoia and shame. But unlike all of us, this is the sum total of what they experience. What would – for a well person – be a momentary thought, a fleeting apprehension, a passing perspective, forms the basis of their whole self-assessment and outlook. They are gripped where most of us are merely touched. They cannot take a break; they cannot look at things from another angle or give themselves and existence the benefit of the doubt. Every morning, they wake up haunted by the same appalling notions: that they have done something irredeemably wrong, that they are irrevocably ugly, that they are comprehensively hateful, that there are enemies everywhere who are right now plotting against them, that they are going to come to an awful end.

All of us will think these sorts of things sometimes, especially when we are tired. But a healthy mind has a vigorous way of ushering in new, redemptive concepts, sometimes within seconds. A gentle, kindly creativity is applied to dilemmas and pains: yes, there might be a mistake, but it doesn't have to be the end; not everyone might be a friend but can there really be enemies everywhere? Perhaps we aren't the most beautiful person, but we have a right to take our place among others.

We might define mental illness as a failure in the capacity to be kind to ourselves. The mentally ill person tyrannically creates an internal theatre in which there is no room for forgiveness, no gentleness to self, no ability to move on, no capacity to introduce less vindictive concepts, no ray of light. The slightest benevolent idea has to be – according to a silent law – ruthlessly strangled at birth.

This gives us a clue as to the likely cause of this form of suffering: a deficit of love, a lack of a sufficient early experience of close-up attention, calmness, sweetness, hopefulness and sympathy to enable one to dissolve the perils and doubts of adult life.

The mentally ill person is at some level treating themselves the way they were formerly treated by others. Their relentless self-laceration is a version of the whipping they received at the hands of a caregiver or parent. They hate themselves as bitterly as they were hated.

Such a diagnosis points us logically to a solution: a reparative kind of love, delivered often enough, intensely enough, reliably enough, convincingly enough that it eventually stands a chance of piercing through the defences of cruelty and puts up a plausible opposition to the chorus of voices of doom and revulsion – a love that might come from a partner, a friend, a therapist or a still-robust-enough part of the sufferer's own mind.

We begin to work our way out of the cavern of mental illness when we can take on board the particularity and unfairness of our self-punishing ways – and allow ourselves to trust in the possibility of a kindness to ourselves that we have until now been too stricken and scared to tolerate.

Why things may need to get worse before they can get better

Our lives are often less than they could be because we are – strangely – too good at making things just about bearable for ourselves. We are experts at endurance, we are copers, we are masters of self-reliance.

Inside, there may be a lot of trouble brewing: intense regret or self-hatred, fear or paranoia. But we are so strong; we don't allow ourselves to fall. We have built a massive concrete dome over the arduous material within, which enables us to lead a semblance of a normal life. We can work hard, we look after a family, we are a good friend – and we have a philosophy that goes with our resilience: we are suspicious of self-exploration, we quickly feel that certain ways of thinking are self-indulgent, we may rather bristle (or sigh) at the thought of psychotherapy.

We are stuck in a peculiar position: the very things that help us to maintain equilibrium are also holding us back from properly dealing with the troubles inside us. We have become too good at not thinking of certain things at the expense of vital insights and catharsis.

Our skills are not negligible assets; to dismiss us as merely stoic, as merely repressed, as merely 'defended' is to miss just how important our gritty manoeuvres of mind are. At some point in our lives, early on, it was precisely these skills that enabled us to survive. It was because we could get cleanly out of touch with our emotions; it was because we had the capacity not to depend on anyone; it was because we could put all our hope, trust and energy into our work rather than our relationships; it was because we learnt to think rather than feel that we were able to make it to the next stage and not succumb to otherwise intolerable degrees of loneliness and fear.

The difficulty is that our defence mechanisms now threaten what remains of life. We have been so good at surviving that we cannot get in a position to thrive. We are buckling because we have no calm way to reduce the tension. We are like a soldier who – many years after an armistice – is still holed up in their bunker, knife and gun at the ready, an expert at combat, when their priority should be the arts of connection, calm and joy.

A slightly paradoxical way out of the problem is for our difficulties to grow to such a pitch that they finally overwhelm our defences and thereby force us to come face to face with the reckoning that we have escaped from for too long. The best way to take the lid off our issues may be for them to boil to such a pitch that the lid blows cleanly away.

To make an analogy with physical illness, perhaps the best thing for a damaged organ whose signs of distress we are overlooking is for these to get so intense, we eventually have no option but to collapse in the doctor's surgery.

So too, our mental recovery may have to wait until the time we no longer know how to cope alone and finally have to look beyond our brilliant array of defences – those that gave us survival but never life in the true, rich sense.

Broadening choices

If we step back from the things that make us most unhappy and ask ourselves why we are enduring them, we may reply that – whatever our levels of discomfort – we just have no choice but to suffer. We tell ourselves that certain things are both unfortunate and simply have to be. For example, we have to stay with a partner even though we are unfulfilled; we have to remain in a job even though the people in charge are belittling us; we have to fail at everything we do no matter how hard we strive; there is no option but to passively hate the way we look or the place we live.

Yet in far more cases than we might presume, liberation awaits us if we have the courage to ask a deceptively simple yet pointed and mind-expanding question: do our supposed lack of choices carry any echoes, or repeat any patterns of assumed necessity, that we once faced in childhood? Are there any links between the particular ways we are fixedly unhappy now and the reasons we were unhappy then?

Children lead notoriously constrained lives; they have to inhabit some very narrow spaces indeed. They face all kinds of agonising binary choices. They must obey a cruel caregiver or get the cold shoulder. They must follow the rules at school or suffer ignominy. They have to avoid the envy of an older sibling or get ridiculed. They have to tend to the depression of a beloved caregiver or feel oppressively guilty.

It is bad enough to suffer such constrictions in our early years. But it is of equal or greater pity when – without even noticing what we are doing – we carry these constrictions into our adult lives; when we unconsciously impose curbs on our choices and set limits on our satisfactions where there are no longer any binding reasons for us to do so; when we continue to live in a narrow room even though the door is wide open before us, inviting us to step through.

We deserve to make a list of our present frustrations and griefs and ask ourselves whether we are not being unknowingly dutiful to certain rules that our deep minds have failed to realise no longer apply. Once we consider the matter afresh, perhaps there is no longer any need to be timid in order to appease the jealousy of a caregiver who died a decade ago; perhaps we don't have to associate love with pain again and again, now that we are free to choose partners who could be uncomplicatedly kind. Maybe we don't need to keep being afraid of failure given that the adults we have to deal with won't be able to scare and upset us in the way that certain people did in childhood.

We humans can be loyal to a fault and too lightly extend our allegiances and our piety to situations that didn't ever deserve them. We honour laws that we cannot even see ourselves obeying. Without noticing the harm we are doing to our interests, we may be continuing to sidestep – and failing to make use of – the true and fundamental freedom of adulthood: the freedom to do things differently.

The logic of our 'illogical' behaviours

The world is filled with people – they may be us at times – who appear to keep acting in ways that mysteriously run entirely contrary to their own interests.

Let's consider a range of examples:

- Someone who keeps withdrawing from their romantic partners as soon as emotional intimacy and closeness are options – which ends up reliably destroying one relationship after another.

- Someone talented who nevertheless continuously messes up whenever they face an important challenge at work – and so wrecks any chance of professional advancement.

- Someone who keeps calling themselves a terrible person and suffers dramatically low levels of self-esteem, though they would have so much to feel proud of if only they assessed themselves more fairly.

- Someone who keeps falling prey to hypochondriacal illnesses that make a free and happy life impossible.

- Someone who throws themselves manically into work or household tasks and thereby removes any opportunity for acknowledging their feelings or developing their mind.

- Someone who keeps resorting to attention-seeking behaviour and so annoys people who would have been quite capable of giving them their time if only they had asked for it in sensible ways.

We may step back and wonder: why do these people act in such contradictory and perverse ways? Why do their actions defy logic?

But this is to misunderstand the workings of our psyches. These so-called perverse actions are not at heart unreasonable at all. These violations of logic are not – considered properly – illogical in the least. It's just that they are out of sync. They are happening at the wrong time, in the wrong place, with the wrong people. These are adaptive strategies that have grown maladaptive. They are, each one of them, manifestations of behaviours that once made profound sense – in a world of intensely challenging childhoods that no longer exists.

Let's consider our examples one by one:

- If we happened to have a parent whose affection was unsteady, who drank a lot or who might have tried to take their own life a number of times, how supremely sensible to develop a capacity to go intensely cold whenever an intimate relationship becomes a possibility. This isn't a pathology, this isn't stupidity. It's a survival strategy – all the more impressive if it was devised when we were 5 years old.

- Or if we had a parent who was extremely vengeful and threatened by our success, what imagination to work out that – in order to make it – we needed to keep failing. What a triumph to deduce so early on the life-saving advantages of underperformance.

- If we had a parent who treated us badly, how inventive to choose to hate ourselves rather than rage at them, given that this allowed us to feel in control and maintain a highly necessary illusion that we had a fundamentally good parent; it was just that we needed to try harder.

- Or if we had a caregiver who only loved us when we were unwell, what brilliance to develop a string of somewhat made-up ailments that might have annoyed doctors but offered us a steady route to tenderness.

- Or if our parents divorced and the pain was unbearable, how brilliant to make sure we were so manically busy we would never need to feel very much at all.

- And if our parents were distracted, how admirable to develop ways of guaranteeing that we could secure their attention by continually making a drama or getting into trouble.

The most fruitless and counterproductive behaviours of adulthood all reveal a logic, once we cease to search for this logic in the present. Whenever we consider a so-called neurosis, we need to ask ourselves: was there ever a time when it might have made sense? Was there ever a situation when it belonged to survival, when it would have helped us to get to the next stage, when it provided a way for us to win the love and care we required?

We may then be able to direct considerable compassion – even admiration – at how creative we were in response to our difficulties. But we also have a chance to put in place new behaviours that better suit our present era and aspirations:

- Once upon a time, there was a logic to being walled in and distant; now it means we'll die alone.
- Once, it was logical to fail; now we're sabotaging our way to penury.
- Once, low self-esteem belonged to survival; now it violates the essence of who we are.
- Once, being constantly ill brought love; now it stops us from existing.
- Once, escaping all self-exploration kept us safe; now it prevents us from knowing who we are.
- Once, theatricality brought us attention; now it alienates those who already care for us.

We might think of ourselves as containing a number of younger children who keep acting according to previously worthwhile scripts. We can be gentle with them. They are doing their best. What they propose isn't 'crazy'; it's just inappropriately timed. We need to learn to see the survival strategy that our neuroses embody, accept how unnecessary they now are and recognise how much we can and should let go of them – with gratitude for the creativity they contain and for the safety they once offered. We should beware of ever dismissing our self-harming behaviours as meaningless. We should learn to search for their purpose, identify it, and then be kind enough to ourselves to discard it in the name of protecting the person we now need to become.

Learning to be good; remembering to be bad

One of the foremost concerns of devoted parents has traditionally been to try to teach their children – from an early age – how to be good, the assumption being that only on the basis of a close appreciation of manners, propriety and polite conduct does anyone stand a chance of a decent life. It's in the pursuit of such goodness that parents will energetically school their children to say please and thank you, to be generous with their toys when friends come around, to ask adults how their day has been, to look people in the eye and to pull frequent smiles.

This clearly has a host of surface advantages, but a curious discovery of psychology is that if a child is to have any chance of leading a genuinely fulfilled life, as opposed to a merely socially respectable one, then they must be allowed a period in which to learn something yet more important than goodness: how to be unrestrictedly and unashamedly 'true' to themselves, which might include such relatively 'bad' behaviour as not saying that something was delicious when it wasn't, not pretending to want to share their toys when they have no wish to, not disguising that they are in a very bad mood when they are and bursting into tears of rage when something feels very sad and hopeless. The path to being real has to pass through a stage of being allowed to experience oneself as no less complicated and difficult than one is. There may, according to this philosophy of child rearing, be a yet more important skill to pick up than goodness, namely authenticity.

This isn't to deny a role for some well-judged fakery a little later on, by the time school starts and friendship groups form. We all need – of course – to learn how to put on a mask in order to function socially. We need to know how to say that something is delicious or fun when it isn't and to stay quiet in meetings even though we disagree with what is being said; these moves belong to the art of survival. But we are not, here, referring to the necessary deployment of a cautionary degree of tact. What is at issue is how much we have – somewhere in our pasts – been allowed to understand who we really are and what we want, in all the more complicated and dark aspects of these terms.

A comprehensively loving parent allows room for the full reality of their child to be witnessed. They do not take fright at the thought that, far from having given birth to an angel, they are dealing with a complete human being, that is, someone who will (in their youthful imaginations) be sometimes greedy, destructive, unkind, vicious, proud, interested in scratching another's eyes out and in making a mess of everything – as well as someone who knows, in other moods, all about love and self-sacrifice and sweetness and empathy. To curtail a child's reality too early on, to insist on good manners from day one, to coerce the child into a raft of false manoeuvres and emotions they don't believe in or relate to isn't ultimately doing the child or society any favours – for what it will lead to are damned up emotions, a disconnection between what they feel and what they are and unnecessary degrees of shame for experiencing desires that cannot be wished away. The child who has been civilised too soon grows up into that problematic character, the preternaturally good boy or girl who knows all about how to please others but whose personality lacks vigour, truthfulness and humour and who suffers from continual unnecessary degrees of embarrassment about pieces of their psyche that they have been forced to disavow in the name of being loved by those they depended on. They cannot get cleanly angry for a while when it would help everyone if they could; they cannot bear to acknowledge key bits of their sexuality; they are stricken by guilt for merely being human.

The emergence of a person who knows how to accept themselves, fathom their depths, be creative and properly kind relies on courage on the part of parents and caregivers. There can be so much fear that one is bringing up an amoral savage that one overlooks the importance of bringing up an unfrightened soul who can admit to a maximum of who they are. The truly privileged child is one who has not had to become someone else in order to enjoy the love and protection they were owed.

Manic rebellion; manic conformity

There are two types of people who are widely known and have far harder lives than they should: the manic rebel on the one hand, the manic conformist on the other.

The rebel might have spent the greater part of their life in protest against authority. At school, they will have kept upsetting the teachers and failed their exams, they won't have followed any prescribed path in their career, they will have loudly scorned every popular idea, they will bristle whenever they encounter the slightest regulation or rule, they will automatically set themselves up against any convention and seem to generate upset and offence wherever they go.

Then there is the manic conformist who seems, on the surface, as if they couldn't be more different. This person smiles all the time, they agree with everything that is said, they do everything that's expected, they anticipate everyone else's needs, they seem never to attract attention and carefully obey every available rule.

But however different these types might appear, both are wrestling with the same dilemma. Both are struggling and failing to adjudicate between their own needs and those of society. If we can then posit a childhood story for these types, both will have missed out on the privilege of being loved for themselves and then shown a tolerable route to succumbing to the wishes of others. Both will have faced a world in which key parents and caregivers wanted them to obey before they had been kind enough to let them be who they were.

The two types will have responded to this harshness in different ways. The rebel will have needed to protect their fragile sense of self by rejecting demands of any sort from the outside. Their reality will so little have been honoured when they were small that any subsequent demand – that they knuckle down for an exam or keep quiet for a few hours – will then inwardly have been experienced as an intolerable threat to their integrity.

The manic conformist, meanwhile, will have responded to their deprivation in a diametrically opposite way. For them, any flouting of any rule will be felt as a prelude to a withdrawal of affection and the onset of disaster. So little were they seen and cherished that any risk of displeasing another person will register as psychologically impossible.

Both types have been denied a quality essential to mental health: that we be allowed to be real and complicated, to displease in the name of expressing something essential to ourselves. In a balanced adult life, we can pay lip service to society – and we can stage intelligent, self-protective protests against collective idiocies and hidebound ideas. We neither need to thumb up our noses to everything nor to smile when nothing is funny.

If we can do some of this on a good day, it's a sign that – without our remembering – someone showed us a wise path between our own requirements and the legitimate demands of the world. They spared us from a life of fruitless rebellion or of equally fruitless plastic smiles.

Secret parental inheritances

We are so used to imagining that a parent's role is to help their child with the difficulties of life that we overlook the extent to which – in secret – many parents are constantly asking their children to do some fairly fundamental favours for them. An unlucky child may spend as much effort unknowingly parenting their parent as they do attending to their own developmental needs.

For example, a parent may need the child to help them to feel that they are capable and useful – and may hold back a child from their independence so that they can keep having a sense that they have a role.

Or a parent may need a child to get a certain sort of result at school so that they can feel clever and prestigious.

Or – more darkly still – a parent may need a child to fail and underperform so that they can feel powerful and successful by comparison.

Or they may need to bully and humiliate their child so that they can feel strong and invulnerable and be certain that they are no longer the fragile person they are terrified of re-encountering.

What is unresolved in a parent has a tragic habit of showing up again as a live dilemma in a child's life. The parent who is confused about their sexuality is likely to bequeath an anxiety about sexual orientation to their child. An adult who is continually worried about their status will surreptitiously communicate a panic in this area to their offspring. We end up inheriting not just photo albums or money from our parents but also feelings of insecurity, hopelessness, self-doubt, fury or sexual turmoil.

Because these emotional inheritances are passed down invisibly, we benefit from stepping back to ask ourselves a basic question: *what were the key things that my parents were likely to have been struggling with in themselves when I was small?* It's an unusual question which little in family life prepares us for. But there will be clues all around, nevertheless. We might sense accurately enough that perhaps a parent was trying to deal with a feeling of intellectual inferiority or of social insecurity. They might have felt anguished about the claims of love on the one hand and of sex on the other. They might have been trying to resist feeling too much after a childhood trauma. They might have felt unacceptable and overlooked in favour of an older sibling.

Our parents, perhaps out of kindness, will not have let on about this. They might not even have been aware that this was what they were dealing with. But it's in the nature of the laws of family life that their neuroses will become ours.

We can spend the greater part of our lives trying – without knowing we're doing this – to solve the problems handed to us in silence by our parents: we're working out how to feel intellectually secure, how to avoid sexual fear, how to have sufficient status. We're trying to find ways of life and solutions that would have saved them.

We may want to get as far away from our parents as possible; we'll do this most effectively when we can figure out which of their problems live on inside us.

The fragile parent

Because there is such an obvious power imbalance between little children and their parents, and because pride and concerns for dignity get in the way of self-awareness, we're apt to miss the curious way in which certain parents rely on their children's approval in order to feel good about themselves – and may easily lose confidence in their abilities if such support is not forthcoming. We may think that an adult couldn't possibly need a small child to buttress their sense of worth, but many fragile parents seem covertly to require that their child be thrilled and delighted by their efforts – and will severely punish and shame one who isn't.

Imagine a parent who sets out to make an apricot tart for their child for teatime. As they assemble the ingredients, they imagine the pleasure in their offspring's eyes once this complicated creation appears from the oven, smelling of moist fruit and sweet pastry. But also imagine the psychic blow when the tart is ready and, far from putting on a scenario of grateful beneficence, the 3-year-old child starts bawling mysteriously, says they hate the cake, throws their cup on the floor and shouts that they want the other parent – the one who is at work or has been watching TV all afternoon – for company.

No one would be delighted, but there are parents for whom this kind of rejection, and others like it, ends up being far too much. No humour is possible; the offence to their sense of integrity is momentous. They need – in order to keep going – a child who will give them a stream of active signs of admiration, a child who will be able to tell jokes, sing to them, do handstands for them and think them heroic and miraculous.

Yet there are children who – for a range of their own reasons – don't emerge from the womb able to deliver this kind of ego reinforcement. Perhaps, as newborns, they don't take well to the breast. They might have colic or an infection of some kind. Later on, they might, by nature, be a little introverted or aloof and wary of a stern parent. They might take more time than most to learn to read or speak and not look as immediately adorable as some youngsters.

The fragile parent who isn't ready for such blows will turn against the child for reminding them of insufficiencies in themselves that they are secretly in flight from. Oppressed by the sense that there may be something amiss with them (both in their role as carer and as a human more broadly), the adult may push the sense of condemnation back onto the child. In a bid to expel their sense of wrongness, they may weave a narrative that this child has no manners, this child is envious, this child is not too clever, this child is strange ...

Tarred by such a story, the unfortunate offspring then grows up with a pervasive sense of self-hatred. They can't put their finger on why exactly; they just know they somehow haven't measured up.

To free ourselves from self-hatred, we may have to accept the initially very odd-sounding idea that a parent several times our size once felt intensely threatened by us, that we managed – without having any such intention – to wound their pride and attack their delicate self-confidence. There was never anything wrong with us; the parent was – beneath their outward bluster and show of importance – more infantile than we were.

We might feel sorry for them when we can manage it – and along the way vow not to have a child of our own until we are resolved enough about our own merits not to have any urgent need for them to adore us back.

Sadism and masochism

Two of the strangest but most powerful aspects of our psychology are drives we refer to as *sadism* and *masochism*. Sadism is understood as an enjoyment in causing others to suffer, whereas masochism is an enjoyment in receiving ill-treatment from others. Though commonly associated with sexual scenarios, these drives operate in all areas of life: at the office or in the schoolyard as much as in the bedroom or the dungeon. Unfortunately, much of what humans do is, in the end, explicable only with recourse to these two melancholy concepts. Which begs enquiry: why do we seem to delight in inflicting suffering or, even more strangely, take satisfaction in enduring it?

The best way to understand the phenomena is to view them as attempts to deal with an earlier intolerable experience of fear, cruelty or unkindness. Before anyone winds up either a sadist or a masochist, they have first been a victim. Subsequent behaviours are a reflection of the mind's concerted attempts to find a way out of a naked encounter with pain. Masochists and sadists are both trying to ensure that they will survive what once felt like it might annihilate them.

The sadist hits on the more straightforward move. Having received cruelty, they conclude that the best way to escape its shadow is to be cruel to somebody else. The poison is redirected outwards. The former terrified child becomes a terrifying adult. Implicitly, the sadist believes that there are only two roles available – victim or perpetrator – and that their best chances of never again ending up as the former is to ensure that they are always the latter. Cruelty promises to buy protection. Sadists can't believe in a world without nastiness (their life stories tell them as much); they just want to make sure they will mete it out rather than receive it.

Masochists have – like sadists – also been the victims of cruelty. Like sadists, they are also in flight from defencelessness. But their method of adaption is more roundabout. A sense of weakness, real or imagined, holds them back from attempts to persecute others. And yet they still need some psychological way of alleviating the memory of suffering – and so hit upon what could almost be labelled an ingenious idea.

They decide that they will henceforth *choose* suffering rather than have it forced on them; they opt to turn a necessity into something akin to a choice. They do to themselves, in their own time, what the world once shocked them to their core by doing to them at a moment of its choosing. Once they had no option but to be bullied by their family; now they go out in active search of mean-minded partners whom they can unconsciously tell will deny them tenderness and care. Once they were told by others that they were worthless and undeserving; now whenever they succeed, they tame their anxieties by cutting themselves down to size by their own hands; they destroy their chances of happiness before anyone else has the chance to do it for them when they are innocent and unprepared. They are assiduous in spoiling every opportunity for contentment and harmony. It may not be easy, but it feels like their first home, and this time, they've at least gone there of their own volition.

Sometimes, the rigmarole turns sexual: a masochist whose parent betrayed them might carefully choreograph a scenario in which they witness their partner making love to a third party. Once loss was imposed, now it happens at their precise behest; they choose the betrayer, they pick out the torture instruments, they decide when they are going to be spat on.

To liberate ourselves, we need to find our way back to the pain that lies behind our behaviours: the bullying we received, the hurt we suffered, the losses that devastated us. And then we should do something we have until now avoided: mourn what we have gone through. We should exchange pain for sorrow. We should cry for what we have had to endure, not ask anyone else – it might be a stranger or, as regrettably, ourselves – to suffer any further. We should restrict pain to the past rather than offering it an indefinite future.

Parents who won't let their children grow up

One might think parents who had spent close to a couple of decades ministering to their children would in time be markedly keen to get them off their hands in order that they might enjoy some remaining years of peace, a clean house and the long-deferred freedom to pursue their own goals. But this would be to underestimate just how much certain parents are – in privacy – relying on their children to satisfy a range of emotional needs with which they are struggling: the need to feel powerful, to have an audience, to play a role, to exist.

These are not necessarily desires that are easy to own up to. Rare is the parent who can cleanly reveal to their child that their maturity – which the child might ardently have fought for over many years – poses a grave threat to their integrity, which would be better assured if the child could, somehow, agree to remain in a cot for the rest of their lives.

In order to delay the moment of abandonment, parents may institute a variety of covert interventions. A parent may develop a psychosomatic illness just as the child is getting ready to go to university – ensuring that the child will either need to stay at home or will never feel entirely free in their minds as they move away.

A parent whose relationship with their partner is not giving them the emotional support they so desperately need may set themselves up against any boyfriend or girlfriend who is brought home – in an attempt to keep their child in the role of proxy husband or wife.

Or a parent may suddenly remove an offer of a loan on which the child had been relying on to advance.

Or a parent may alternate between being approving and suddenly withdrawing affection, exciting in the child a morbid dependency and need to confirm a love of which they can never be certain. There are parents who have cannily worked out that the best way to keep a child close isn't to adore them unconditionally (this will only lead to being taken for granted) – it's to leave them continually unsure that they have any kind of safe place in their fickle hearts.

Or, most mysteriously, a parent may rattle a child's mind by implying that the wish to separate isn't compatible with being kind or good. It doesn't take much for a child to develop a sense that their freedom has come at too high a price for the person they adore. The child might suffer a breakdown, ostensibly regretted by everyone, yet hugely beneficial to a 'nurse' who now needs to be on duty 24/7, much as they would have been in the earliest days.

It's an immense privilege to be looked after tenderly. It's an even greater privilege to be – at the right moment – benignly abandoned: to receive no phone calls for many days (or even weeks), to not be asked if one is keeping warm or has enough cake left (one is and does), to have one's partners enthusiastically endorsed and to be able cleanly, for a while, to forget where one came from.

The complicated truth is that a good parent always needs their child as much as, perhaps more than, the child needs them; a truly helpful parent is sure never to let on.

The roots of obsessive thinking

For some of us, today – like every day – will mean another case of immersing ourselves, from the moment we wake up, in a by-now very familiar set of painful thoughts. We will dwell, once again, on how awful we look and, more particularly, how our nose is repulsively proportioned relative to the rest of our face. We will think, once again, of a website we inadvertently visited twelve years ago and how the police might be preparing to close in on us and make an arrest. We will think, once again, of how several of our neighbours (especially the people upstairs) might be colluding to ruin and disgrace us. Or we will think, once again, of something we said to a colleague that we fear they misconstrued, and which may well lead them to seek disciplinary action against us at any moment.

These thoughts may ostensibly be about a variety of topics but beneath the surface, they have two features in common: they are about something appalling we feel we are or have done. Or they are about something appalling we fear that others are about to do to us. We are the victims of one of the cruellest and most remorseless of all mental afflictions: obsessive thinking.

Crucially, obsessive thinking is not – despite the linguistic proximity – to be confused with thinking per se. It certainly looks on the surface as though the obsessive thinker is thinking a lot. All day, they might be drawing up dense charts and jotting down intricate matters in a notebook. They might want to leave a party early or escape family life in order to go to their room to 'think'. They might have become near world experts in plastic surgery or police surveillance techniques or in an area of employment law. They would be able to tell you everything about tracking devices, post-operative skin treatments and the minute-by-minute developments in a specific aspect of the media agenda.

Their cogitation may be extreme, but we may still want to resist calling any of this thinking. As obsessive thinkers, we are not making progress through anything of note; we're not advancing through a dilemma; we're not clearing up a priority. We are thinking in order not to think. By which is meant, we are using one kind of thought to ward off another. We are employing obsessive thinking as a defence against thinking more laterally and emotionally about who we are and what has happened to us; against knowing ourselves properly.

To try to break the agonising loops in our minds, we might try to ask ourselves a deceptively simple-sounding question: if we could not think about our chosen topic, if we were to be debarred from returning to our favoured theme, what might we think about? What other thoughts might lie behind or to the side of our entrenched ritualised preoccupations?

Our minds are unlikely to yield a neat answer. But we can hazard a generalisation: if we could not think about our obsessive topic, we would most likely need, in one way or another, to feel intensely, overwhelmingly sad, lonely, desperate or bereft. Behind the monomaniacal thoughts about cameras or data packets or legal processes or social media, there is almost always an extremely frightened, isolated, unloved child who long ago could not bear to inhabit their own experience. Obsessive patterns of thinking have attached themselves remorselessly to the walls of the mind in order to prevent a tragic re-encounter with an early, highly vulnerable and hurt version of oneself.

In a bid for relief, we should dare – for once – to risk not returning to our usual themes and instead, while conceding that this is what we might be doing, stop running. We should pause where we are and leave our secondary thoughts time to catch up with us. We should put down our fixations and let the waves of our background grief and fear wash over us. However tightly we have associated our problems with our favoured topic of scrutiny, there has almost certainly long been something bigger, older and more tragic that we have been unable to look at: that we were maltreated by a caregiver; that our parents chronically preferred a sibling to us; that our father humiliated us repeatedly to overcome his shame at his own sexual abuse.

We have, at an unconscious level, made a desperate choice to think ill of ourselves or to worry about plots against us, in order to impose a degree of logic on an otherwise impossibly confounding early experience of neglect or betrayal: to an indigestible experience of untrustworthiness, to a failure of love.

Our minds may gradually have an opportunity to grow less consumed by obsessive thoughts the more we can interpret our preoccupations as symptoms of other concerns we are in flight from, the more we can give up our feelings of persecution, unacceptability and guilt in favour of a sadder, slower, older truth about ourselves: that we were very badly let down indeed.

How psychotherapy might truly help us

There can be considerable confusion as to why exactly it might be helpful to visit a psychotherapist. Typically, we might suppose that the benefit lies in the chance to speak with a friendly person, to have a shoulder to cry on, or to be listened to with sympathy.

Yet however helpful these elements might be (and at times they might be truly critical), the primordial benefit, that which can make psychotherapy transformative rather than merely consoling, arguably lies somewhere slightly different: in the opportunity it affords us to play out our madness under close observation.

All of us are – on the basis of our complicated childhoods – the heirs of some deeply distorted assumptions about ourselves and the people around us. We may believe, for example, that anyone who gets to know us well will be revolted by us; or that succeeding must mean losing the love of people we rely on; or that it's our duty to look after our partners however little they care for us; or that we need to be hugely funny and entertaining at every moment to win others' favour.

Normal life typically goes by far too fast for such distortions to come cleanly to light. No one quite sees what we are up to or cares to tell us generously and precisely – partly because we play out our eccentricities in such varied locations and around people with intense compulsions and burdens of their own. There is – day to day – simply too much static for us to be able to make an unsullied assessment of our distinctive follies.

The beauty of psychotherapy is that we will, without trying, end up rehearsing around the therapist many of the same peculiarities we manifest in the world outside. But with one big difference: now, at last, someone is watching with maximal maturity, sanity and impartiality. They're not trying to raise a child with us or run a business with us or persuade us to go for a meal with their mother. They're not resentful about something we did a year ago and don't have (or shouldn't have) intense immature needs of their own to play out (this will go on in their private lives). All they are doing is listening in a calm, personally resolved way to the movements of our psyches. They can thereby provide a clinically pristine petri dish in which the antics we commonly manifest in the noisy, smudged realm outside can be isolated and addressed.

In a quiet room with a person who says hardly anything to us about themselves and who behaves in a mild, moderate, kindly manner, a place in which we're not trying to do anything practical or logistical, in which there are no interruptions, the warps in our behaviour will be easier to track: our insistence that everyone hates us, or our desire to seduce strangers as a way of gaining attention, or our fear that we're being annoying when we are vulnerable, or our desire to help people at our own expense – all these can come into view. Is it really true – a therapist can ask – that I am only interested in you because of your appearance?

Or that every setback is going to end in catastrophe? Or that men and women are fated never to understand one another? Or that I am going to abandon you if you don't impress me?

We have a chance to get to know our distorted apprehensions of existence, to understand what these owe to the particular challenges of our pasts and to appreciate how they are rendering our relationships with ourselves and the people around us more taxing than they need to be.

We may come away from an experience of therapy with a newfound sense (which might feel very disorienting at first) of what it would be like to walk with somewhat diminished terror and self-hatred through a more innocent and ghost-free world.

II.

Relationships

Relationships as a route to self-knowledge

One reason why relationships are valuable is that they enable us to know ourselves better; being part of a couple can help us to understand who we are.

With a partner alongside us, we can – to an unusual extent – be properly seen. Someone is there late at night and first thing in the morning; someone can hear our private fears and uncensored joys. Someone can witness us without our masks on, in gleeful or despairing moods, when we say things we generally don't say, when we are no longer playing a role.

As a result, some of what we keep missing about ourselves can come to light. Our partners may see what we no longer can see, both what is adorable and what is more perplexing and difficult. They might, for example, remind us that we've told that anecdote (three times) before, or that purple doesn't suit us. They can tell us that we've overreacted to a problem at work, or that we've placed our trust in an envious friend. They can suggest where we should not worry so much and where it would be wise to fret more. Their responses give us a chance to grow slightly less obtuse, haughty and peculiar.

But despite the potential of love to function as a route to self-knowledge, in practice, we are likely to walk away from our relationships with most of our delusions intact. Some of our problem comes down to pride. We cannot find it in our hearts to forgive our lovers for catching sight of material that fails to accord with what we want to be true of ourselves. We come to love hoping to be admired; they note that we aren't always very funny, that our novel is patchy, that we are prone to self-pity, that we lose our temper too fast, that we have disappointing household habits or never properly say what we mean.

Far from using these bits of difficult news as goads for self-improvement, we find it substantially easier to get insulted, to say that a partner is being 'mean' or 'inconsiderate' and to block our ears. We fall back on a noxious but highly prevalent idea about love: that, in a good relationship, no one should be trying to 'change' anyone. Presumably because we are perfect enough already. Or else because all our faults should be forgiven, as they were when we were infants. True love means – we are told – not wanting to alter a single thing about someone. Were we to share among friends that we had ended a relationship on the basis that a partner was 'trying to change us', we could count on receiving a lot of sympathy and being widely commended for our bravery.

Yet given how monstrously imperfect we all are, true kindness should never mean abandoning a person to their eccentricities, their losses of perspective, their unjustified fury, their unexplored hurts or their questionable dress sense. It should mean helping them – gently but frankly – to learn more about who they presently are in the name of the better person they might one day become.

The fault doesn't lie only with us as the recipients of feedback; we tend to usher our partners towards self-knowledge with unhelpful brusqueness and anger. Whereas the gossamer-thin human ego begs for a tone of reassurance and patience, we allow irritation and fear to cloud the important truths we are trying to impart. We attempt to instruct our partners in vital facts about themselves last thing at night or the moment they get home in a rainstorm. We are so scared of what they don't know of themselves, we destroy any chance they might have of patiently coming to understand it. We grow too angry to remember that we are trying to help someone to evolve, not punish them for having fallen short of our hopes. At worst, despite fine intentions, we give up after only a few minutes of measured conversation, call them a 'shithead', slam the door and shout that they are as bad as their mother or father. A good deal of what we say in anger may – ironically – be entirely true. It's just that no one has ever learnt anything about themselves in conditions of belittlement and humiliation.

In order to capitalise on the potential of relationships, we should be stricter on the ground rules:

1. We should start by insisting – contrary to the romantic script – that true love is entirely compatible with attempts to teach people who they are and how they might improve. The only people whom we don't want to change are those we don't care about. We should re-imagine love as a privileged arena in which two people will – with immense kindness and tact – try to hold a mirror to each other's most difficult and broken sides in the name of growth and progress towards psychological adulthood.

2. At the same time, huge attention should be paid to the way we share our insights. We must become the most willing of students and the kindest of teachers. We should strive to only divulge tricky things when we aren't smarting from our contact with them. We need to strike, lightly, when the iron is cold.

3. We should soften our verdicts with recourse to words like 'perhaps' and 'maybe'. We should say we feel that they 'may be missing something', not that we (and our therapist) are certain of their insanity. We should remember that emotional truths can only ever be heard in an atmosphere of intimate safety.

4. We should be wary of how often our own histories may give us a false impression of who our partners are. We may be far from the experts we think. We are highly likely at times to mistake their motives for those of figures from our past; we can be far too quick to imagine, with unjust alarm, that we have married our mother or father.

Most relationships collapse because – in the end – two people didn't want to know more about themselves; because the knowledge was too hard and because the way it was divulged was too tough. Given how much precious psychological information every relationship throws up, we should do ourselves the honour of using it intelligently and adroitly; we should share our hard-won insights with unlimited tenderness and strive to hear them – always – with trust, curiosity and courage.

How do you respond when love is reciprocated?

An unusually effective way of gauging how much kindness we have for ourselves is to take a measure of how we responded the moment we learnt that our affections for someone were reciprocated, the moment when a person whom we'd had our eye on for a time shed their reserve and revealed a reciprocal enthusiasm.

Which of the following might we be tempted to use to complete the sentence: *When someone I like likes me back ...*

I am so pleased

Some of us have been blessed enough in our psychological histories to be able to hold on to two deceptively simple and yet, in reality, extremely complex possibilities: that we are – on balance – worthy enough of being liked. And that a person who likes us may, overall, be decent, kind, clever and a fitting recipient of our affections. That we can think this way is not merely a personal achievement; it's evidence that much has gone well in our pasts. We can think this way now because, many years ago, someone we respected rewarded what they perceived as worthwhile in us. They were reliable in their care. We learnt that they would be here again tomorrow and the day after; it appeared to be safe to place them at the centre of our world. We trust now because, in a highly vulnerable state, we were able to trust then. We have enough ballast to survive a failure. We can withstand the anxieties of hope – and dare to give mutual love a chance. We have passed the single greatest test of emotional maturity.

I worry there's been a mistake

We may have no particular trouble admiring people; we may be quite comfortable quietly pining for someone across a library or on a train or at the office. The difficulty comes when the unfortunate target of our desire decides they like us back. Their interest scratches at a very sore region of our psyches. Everything in our past has taught us that we can't measure up to those we admire, that no one we like ever turns our way, that we cannot both love and be loved. Back then, however hard we tried – at school, in sport or at the piano – it was (let's imagine) our sibling they liked more, or all the things that preoccupied them at work and prevented them from coming home to spend time with us. We may be pleased by news of reciprocation, but we are first and foremost extremely worried. The positive verdict can't be real, and the error is going to come to light. Nothing so beautiful is possible. Our admirer must be on the verge of perceiving some of what so disappointed our early caregivers – and their responses will be similarly sharp and devastating. Given the scale of our anxiety, it may just be easier to say we're busy or not answer any of their messages – to hurry along the blow that we are certain is, in any case, coming our way.

I go off them at once

There is another response, this time more outwardly critical, to being liked when we lack affection for ourselves: to decide that our admirer cannot be who we imagined they were. They cannot be the accomplished, kind or good person we had pictured, given that they have just exhibited the bad taste and poor practical judgement of approving of someone like us. How could we allow them to think better of us than we think of ourselves? We aren't so much worried about being found out as disgusted by the weakling who has seen fit to bestow their fondness on a misshapen target. We steal a march on self-doubt by pre-emptively labelling our seducer a fool and an oddball. We may be theoretically pleased that someone has fallen for us, but we can't for a moment continue to rate their intelligence or – indeed – prevent a feeling of nausea at the mere mention of their name.

The crucial detail is that this multiple choice has not involved any lover in particular. We cannot – as we normally do in the rush of life – attribute our response to a given set of qualities or flaws in a person in front of us. We therefore have a chance to see, more clearly than we typically can, that a predominant share of our response to a potential partner is determined by our pasts. Our decision to trust or distrust, to worry or to feel sick, has little to do with the complicated, independent being across the table from us suggesting a walk or another coffee. The way we answer tells us about our experiences in childhood, not about our trajectories in the dating world. This offers hope by highlighting how unfair we may – until now – have been to reality. We may be far freer than we think to love and be loved once we relegate our first emotional responses to the difficult pasts that generated them.

Beyond defensiveness

The trait we should perhaps be keenest to vanquish in any attempt to become that most elusive but most commendable of beings, a proper emotional grown-up, is defensiveness – a pattern of response that lies behind more broken relationships, distraught families and dysfunctional workplaces than any other.

What defines the defensive person is their recourse to demoralising aggression, denial and irritation in the face of any unwelcome pieces of information about their character or habits. Sometimes, what we are trying to tell them will be discounted on the basis that we ourselves are not, in all areas, invariably without fault – and therefore we have no right to try to improve anyone else (neatly missing that we only ever have insight into the fragilities of others because we are not personally beyond reproach). Or else our remarks will be undermined by a cynicism as to our motives: we might be told that we are only saying something because we are jealous or sexually threatened or inadequate or have a pre-existing bias against a certain race, class or gender, anything other than the more troubling notion that we might be trying to share an insight because we care.

Alternatively, our analysis might be deflected with an appeal to an imagined arbiter or judge who, though not in the room, would adjudicate matters from a very different and far wiser standpoint. Without time for opinion polls or interviews, we are told that 'Your friends wouldn't agree ...', 'Your mother doesn't think so ...' or, more grandly and definitely, that 'No one thinks that way nowadays ...'

Then, if the mood grows yet more tense, we might be told that we are unkind for speaking as we have: 'After all I've done for you ...', 'When I've been so nice all weekend ...', 'When I nursed you through your cold ...' There might be an appeal to etiquette: the point that's being made might well be interesting. In theory, the person we are speaking to is open to it, but they won't explore it now because the way it's been phrased is too 'rude', 'hostile' or 'overly agitated' (and won't be considered until, and unless, we have calmed down – a rule with an exceptional power to excite us all over again). Lastly, to ensure that any chance of dialogue can properly be terminated, we may be buttressed into silence by the hammer of weakness: 'I'm too upset to hear any more of this ...' 'You're going to give me a heart attack if we continue ...'

To work our way out of the cul-de-sac, we need to start with an understanding of the true cause and underlying fuel of defensiveness, namely, self-ignorance. We flare up in response to the comments of others because we are operating, deep down, with an unclear picture of who we are. We are angry because we have no reliable map of our virtues and vices, because we are oscillating between a brittle faith in our accomplishments and a bleak terror of our flaws.

The self-aware person has overcome any such uncertainty. They will long ago have exchanged perfectionism and self-loathing for a more stable and judicious assessment of their natures, as much in their positive as in their negative dimensions. They will have gone around their minds at their own pace, without the intimidating presence of an angry partner or an accusatory colleague, and made a proper audit of their psyches. And there will, as a result, be nothing that their worst enemy can tell them that they have not – with realism – either bravely taken on board or serenely rejected already.

Some of what they have recognised will be truly sombre: yes, they really are quite silly. Unfortunately, they truly are very bad in bed. Lamentably, they haven't necessarily been a good parent. Horrifically, they have aged a lot ... But these ideas are now well known. They have been raked over and digested. There isn't any need to insist spitefully or nervously on their opposites.

At the same time, self-knowledge sets useful limits on how much we need to despise ourselves. The self-aware explorer will recognise that they are imperfect in so many ways, but they will also know that they genuinely aren't wholly monstrous either; they truly have never set out to harm anyone, they don't want to triumph over their enemies, they sincerely have no interest in undermining their friends, they have never stolen anything ...

We will be past defensiveness when every nagging insecurity that we had previously banished to the periphery of consciousness has been pulled squarely into the centre and there examined and defused; when we have considered every harrowing possibility: that we are indeed a poor friend, a dismal worker, a narrow-minded traveller – and, overall, a thoroughly short-sighted and dim-witted human. Thereafter, we might hear much that is negative, but we'll never need to bite in response to a remark because either it will be false, and therefore can be discarded without fluster, or else it will be true, and we'll be able to remain even-tempered because we'll be as aware as our angriest opponent of its justice and validity. We'll know who we are – and so will never need to greet a challenging idea about us with weapons again.

Learning to laugh at ourselves

Experience tells us that there is something unusually positive about being someone who can – as we put it – 'laugh at themself'. Equally, there is something distinctly dangerous in a more stony-faced or imperious manner.

The reason has nothing to do with a love of comedy. We're not looking for entertainment pure and simple. What we're fundamentally after is a sign that someone we're interested in knows themselves well enough to have worked out the many ways in which they are likely to prove enraging and disappointing to someone who is forced to live around them. Given that everyone will, at points, prove to be a jerk, we cherish self-deprecating humour as heart-warming evidence that a person might at least be a moderately self-aware, minimally self-justifying, emotionally curious sort of jerk.

There seems to be an enormous difference between people who let us down while angrily denying they have done so and those who madden us and – in their less combative moments – can roundly acknowledge their impossible dimensions; people who might ruin aspects of our lives but have no need to bitterly insist otherwise.

Under the guise of cracking a joke, what the self-deprecating person is in essence doing is letting us know that they can well see what is impossible about them and are, in their way, deeply sorry for the multiple inconveniences that they have generated. They might employ irony to touch on their flaws. They might, for example, hint that they understand how bad they are at organisation by noting that if misplacing things were an Olympic sport, they'd have won and misplaced their medal by now – or at decisiveness by saying that if they were presented with the choice of tea or coffee, they might take a couple of years and some therapy to work out the answer. It's not comic genius and it doesn't have to be. It's about a deft allusion to a knowledge of how much of a trial one can be.

Alternatively, the self-deprecating person might exaggerate their flaws beyond normal measure in order to wryly take on board how truly unusual they might feel. They might acknowledge their reserve and lack of emotion by saying that the UN has asked them to help reverse the melting of the Antarctic ice shelf. Or they might admit to how otherworldly they can seem when they've been absorbed in their work by saying, on emerging from their study, that their intergalactic spaceship and astronaut's suit are waiting for them in the garden.

To become better able to laugh at ourselves, we don't need to learn comic techniques. We need only to make a list of everything that is liable to madden other people about us – our anger, our passivity, our self-pity, our laziness, our sentimentality or our bitterness – and then calmly allude to them through ironic under- or overstatement.

The primary goal is to bring about a release of tension and – in effect – of fear in the face of all the things that may be most troubling and frightening about us. When our audience laugh, they aren't so much amused as relieved. They are being encouraged to know that the person they have to deal with isn't just an idiot, they are – blessedly – a self-aware idiot, an essential, life-saving difference.

We don't need people to be perfect; we need people to know they are imperfect and then not to blame us for our grief and irritation at finding them so. We want self-aware fools, self-aware blockheads, self-aware ingrates. We want people who know they are pricks and, in a small part of their minds, are resolutely intent on evolving into something kinder.

Being upset without knowing it

We might expect that if we were in any significant way annoyed with our partner, we would naturally and spontaneously notice the matter. If they had let us down, if they had failed to respond to our needs, if they'd left us in doubt as to their feelings, we should, without effort, be aware of the problem – and then be able to address it at speed.

But that would be to misjudge quite how opaque and unknown we generally are to ourselves. It isn't in any way inevitable that we register everything that courses through us. Much of what we are isn't experienced; a substantial share of our true emotions fails to make it along the mind's internal labyrinths to conscious awareness. In order for it to do so, we rely on particular encouragement; we require an environment that legitimises our concerns and allows us to remain curious about ourselves, especially when what we feel doesn't accord with prevailing notions of normality or respectability. Small children don't understand a lot about themselves unless there are adults around who can pay attention to their cries of pain. We rely on a rich, nuanced, sympathetic vocabulary from the outside to register things that are going on inside.

We ultimately lack knowledge of what we feel around our partners for a poignant reason: because their power to upset us is so great. Everything they do – or don't do – matters to our state of mind. Our sensitivity threatens to strip us of our independence and reduce us to an intolerable vassal status. Whereas in most areas of grown-up life, we can strive for strength and equanimity, our relationships demand something quite different: that we place ourselves at the mercy of another who can profoundly knock our composure by not smiling broadly enough at one of our minor jokes, someone who can ruin our day by saying 'That's so interesting' in a distracted way, someone who can make us wonder whether we're leading the right life because they fail to hold our hand when we reach out to them in the night.

No wonder we frequently simply discount the evidence of our hurts and admit only to a more composed, narrow and imperturbable range of emotions. How natural that we might suffer a blow to our esteem and then maintain – with outward sincerity – that we are entirely fine, but would prefer some time alone.

An upset that hasn't been acknowledged isn't – unfortunately – any less real for that. It continues to reverberate within us and to demand that its presence be known, showing up in garbled forms as coldness, irritability, illness, addiction to news or pornography, disinterest in sex or openness to affairs. All this because our minds cannot bear to confront the awkward but entirely serious truth that we are weeping inside because, four days ago, our partner forgot to buy us some cherries, or talked about a person at work who makes us jealous, or didn't notice our new haircut.

We should make it easier to understand ourselves by collectively adjusting our sense of what it might be normal to be susceptible to in relationships. We should – at a societal level – alter our impression of our vulnerability to so-called 'small things'. Of course we get upset by everything pretty much all the time. Of course we care infinitely. Of course we surrender the keys to our happiness to the person we love. We should give up the childish notion that adults in relationships can only be expected to respond to one another in robust and reasonable-sounding ways. We should have the insight – and courage – of our true sensitivity.

The need for manners in love

We probably think rather badly of 'good manners': all those *pleases* and *thank-yous* and *how are yous* that were painfully drilled into us in childhood to civilise us, but which have so little to do with who we actually are.

Yet while we may grudgingly accept a certain logic for manners in a few areas – at the office or at a party, for example – the area where the concept truly seems to have no place is love. Nothing sounds quite as unromantic as two lovers who daily strive to be 'polite' with one another; honest, lively, sweet, authentic, of course, but polite? We look to relationships for untrammelled authenticity: here – at last – we will be able to say what we truly think; here – at last – we will no longer need to hedge and walk on eggshells. A loving partner will witness us in our unfiltered reality and endorse us.

But while the longing is understandable, the reality is far from fertile – let alone kind. To be entirely 'ourselves' around someone is a complicated treat we should probably spare anyone we remotely care about, for what this will in reality entail is an uncompromising and bracing encounter with plentiful reserves of ill-temper, selfishness, confusion, infidelity, vindictiveness, foul odours and rage. To be as we genuinely are entails blaming a partner for things they've never done, passing on disappointments that don't belong to them, expressing the full force of verdicts in a way that might pulverise their esteem, pointing out flaws without any care for balance and burping at will. We should – where love is the goal – very much want people not to be who they really are.

Indeed, we might want them to sign up to a basic charter of good conduct, an agreed set of four cast-iron rules for how to behave so as to give love a chance:

1. *Accuracy*

It's in the nature of many moods of distress that their exact causes elude us. Something bad has happened today but, unable to put our finger on exactly what, we may point to the nearest significant (and, importantly, safe) object in view: our partner, perhaps at that moment innocently moving around the kitchen, unaware of what is about to befall them, trying to get through the turmoils of their own brief existence as best as they can. It might have been our boss, a worry about financial security, a glimpse in the mirror or a rivalry with a sibling that has triggered our distemper, but these are hard elements to get clear about, let alone resolve. So it's only natural to focus in on the one person in the vicinity who is forbearing – the one person whom we know has the strength to bear our injustice – and start to tell them that their friends are superficial or that they should probably try to lose weight, thereby acting with some of the poise of a 3-year-old who, struck by a burst of jealousy at a friend with a better toy, screams cathartically, 'I hate Mummy.'

2. *Kindness*

We can be so convinced that kindness is a natural consequence of love that we forget it might be its artificial precondition: that we might – in order to remain in a relationship – need to make certain entirely synthetic and contrived efforts to find gentle and understandable words for our most important truths. There could, of course, be other more direct ways to say what has leapt into our minds: we could use terms like shithead and fuckwit if we liked; we could tell our partner that they're brutish and daft, and these appellations would undoubtedly carry some of the sense of letdown and hopelessness that has afflicted us, but if continuing in a couple is the desired outcome, then we would be wise to go into another room for a time and bite our hand. Manners aren't just a worthless rigmarole; they're founded on the insight that our need for respect is – after food and water – probably our most urgent and non-negotiable requirement.

3. Keep it personal

The temptation, in anger, is to universalise our judgements so as to convey how deeply they strike us. That's why we end up telling our partner that they are – not just in our view, but in their essence, in a way that a court of law or a divine judge would think – cold, selfish, stupid, needy or hypocritical ... It feels so deeply true, but if we're interested in retaining the ear of a person we may want to be thinking of on our deathbed, we'd be better off trying for something more local and conditional: *I feel you might ... Perhaps I get a sense that ... Maybe I've sometimes had the impression that ...* Love thrives on an absence of categoricals.

4. Feeling heard

The law here is brutal: we will not hear until we feel heard. We won't be able to acknowledge the feelings of those who have denied our own. And so, though everything in us is certain that justice is on our side, we must do everything, before we launch forth on any rebuttal, to categorically show that we have listened to our lover's point – by repeating it back to them as faithfully as we can using slightly different words. 'I'm hearing that you don't feel I am doing enough around the house and that's making you wonder whether things are fair in this relationship …' We don't need to do anything practically more complicated, though emotionally tortuous and restrictive, than paraphrase: 'I hear that you're feeling very let down by me because of the way I behaved around your friend and that is reminding you of being belittled last summer when, at your aunt's cabin by the lake, you got the feeling that …' We know so much about what we want to say, but it'll go entirely unheard until we can rehearse what we've just been told.

Manners are undoubtedly agony. Our hatred of them is in no way misfounded. And yet – tragically – it seems that only by limiting our right to free expression, only by restricting liberty, only by disallowing ourselves from being 'who we really are', can we get any closer to what we want: a partner who feels good enough about themselves to be able to acknowledge what matters most to us. Authentic, kind and true relationships may require us to be – far more often than we'd like – substantially affected, stilted and unnatural.

The seductive power of being seen

We might assume that the highest pleasure in relationships would be to be praised and approved of, and that what we are all searching for in love is a visibly-smitten soul who can deliver laudatory homages to us and our many qualities.

But that would be to overestimate how nice eulogies ever feel. Whatever the occasional thrill of a compliment, there is something a great deal more attractive, reassuring and rare about being around someone who knows our faults full well – and yet is able to treat them with patience, charitable humour and compassion. We don't want someone to extol us; we need someone to do something far more difficult: see us as we are and still keep faith.

To be on the receiving end of panegyrics, to hear that we're astounding and adorable most often simply results in feelings of dissociation and alarm; we sense, implicitly, that it can only be a matter of time until our more complicated reality is discovered and deplored. Or else we buy our place on a pedestal at the cost of an eerie loneliness. Rather than be revered, we want to be understood for our reality, namely accepted as being, to a substantial extent, difficult, moody, intemperate, unfair, pained, jealous, anxious and absurd.

That someone should be able to perceive all this about us and not run away, not vilify us, not view our flaws in the worst possible light, not get furious or condemnatory, is the true prize of love; this is what makes us feel genuinely safe and is therefore sincerely romantic.

The most tender thing we might hear from a lover is that we are weird yet interesting, a mess yet vibrant, silly yet charming. We want the deeper reasons behind our flaws to be taken into account. We might delight in someone who can remember that we haven't set out to be nightmarish, we're just in pain; we'd dearly love to be better, we're just often overwhelmed and scared. We want someone to recall that our difficulties have tender orgins. We are like this because our start really did set us particular challenges. We had to struggle against some rare obstacles; those early years were extremely unusual. The loving partner can keep in mind – as we fall into another sulk or panic – that there is a history to our exhausting behaviour and that our best chances of evolving into someone more mature and saner would be if they could refrain from definitively labelling us (as they would in fact have every right to) a big baby or a maddening jerk.

One of the most thrilling eventualities in love is to be called out with kindness, when a partner rolls their irritation into a humorous nickname ('sweet little monster', 'loveable ball of anxiety', 'four-time winner of the Charles Manson award for psychopathy'), directing our gaze to an especially awkward habit of ours without fury. They know our eagerness to be liked by important people, they've noticed our intellectual pretension, they understand how vain we are – and yet, remarkably, they are still here; they have not abandoned us to our vices.

Anyone can – for a time – glorify our existence. The prize is to land on that far more unique and cherishable being: one who knows full well the many ways in which we're awful but, despite the issues, can also bear to remember that we are trying our best, that we seldom do it on purpose and that we are, on balance, probably worth sticking with.

The unreadability of our minds

Few of us explicitly sign up to a belief in the occult art of mind-reading: the view that – possibly with the help of some tarot cards or a Ouija board – one person will be able to peer through another's skull and divine their most elusive thoughts without any words being exchanged.

Nevertheless, we do tend – in a practical sense – very often to behave exactly as though we do trust in such an ideology. We constantly allow ourselves to get extremely frustrated with people for not knowing things that have a very substantial place in our minds, and yet if we stopped to explore the delicate matter, we would realise we had never told them. We sigh repeatedly at the incompetence, short-sightedness, lack of empathy and selfishness of individuals to whom we have never granted any chances to know us properly.

To judge whether we do – despite our professed rationalism – implicitly believe in divination and the telegenic transfer of information between psyches, we should undertake a basic exercise. We should make a list under the heading 'People who frustrate me – and what they don't understand.' It may be rather a long one; there might be room on it for a child who never reads enough, a parent who keeps interrupting our work in the morning, a colleague who doesn't properly update the website or a partner who has horrible shoes or a maddening habit of leaving the kettle pulled away from the wall (we actually like it very close to the sockets).

And then we should ask ourselves a simple but probably profoundly unfamiliar question: 'Have we ever told them about this?' Here, crucially, we don't mean have we ever grunted at them intemperately on our way out of the room, or reflected at length on their incompetence while in the bath or on the train home? We mean, quite literally: have we ever taken somewhere between one and ten minutes to go through in detail – with kindness, patience, humour and politeness – why something that happens to matter very much to us should ideally have some role to play in their own considerations?

If we can't be certain that we have, if we have remained as tight-lipped as we have been furious, though we may not explicitly vaunt our faith in runes and palmistry, we are progressing through existence with some of the esoteric spiritualism of a Madame Blavatsky or George Gurdjieff.

Our hopes have origins that could be seen as almost sweet. Most of us were, at the very start of our lives, the beneficiaries of some astonishing minor acts of mind-reading on the part of our caregivers. They might, in our first six months, have correctly guessed that we were after some milk when we began crying, that the sun was in our eyes when we squinted or that we needed a lie down when we seemed cranky. And it was from these generous acts of empathy that a more pernicious belief then took hold: that anyone who cared about us would henceforth simply know what was going through our distressed minds without us needing to speak, even when the subject at hand might have graduated to the relatively more complex matter of what to do with the Italian tax rebates or how to invoice the Singapore client ahead of the conference.

We have all already spent so many hours marinating in bittersweet reflections on what others have misunderstood about us and the deliberate delight they took in doing so. We should sometimes interrupt the fun with a question of near-Cartesian significance: *did we tell them?*

Other people as a guide to ourselves

We can spend a lot of time wondering what other people might really be thinking: it could be our colleagues, an ex, a parent, a child, a stranger on a train ... We know intuitively that their true thoughts may be rather different from what they imply, but what could really be at play?

There is one tool that we are surprisingly reluctant to make use of in order to penetrate the mystery of others: our own experience. Almost the very last thing we dare to have recourse to is the thought that our opaque acquaintances or friends might, to a substantial extent, resemble us – that what they are most likely to be feeling is a version of what we have felt (but perhaps never quite faced up to feeling) in the quieter corners of our minds. We make astonishingly little use of our private lives when trying to decode the private lives of others.

Our reluctance can be traced back to childhood. To a 5-year-old, the idea that their teacher might, in certain important ways, be similar to them is a profoundly alien thought. If one Saturday morning by chance the child was to spot their teacher in the supermarket in their jogging gear by the cereal, they might be deeply surprised: a teacher – who had only lately been telling them about the history of the Vikings – likes chocolate cornflakes? They are interested in ice cream? They've got headphones? Similar surprise might – many years later – be felt if we saw our doctor at the skating rink, our accountant at the beach or learnt about the sorrows of an airline pilot.

In our response to these professionals, we catch an echo of a broader self-doubting supposition: that other people cannot be quite as we are, and, in particular, that they are unlikely to share in all the vulnerable, extreme, embarrassing, odd or frivolous aspects of our natures.

We think this way because of a fundamental feature of the way we understand humans: we know ourselves from the inside but can know others only from what they choose to tell us, an inevitably much more edited and sober selection. But what if we were to employ ourselves as the leading guide to the intimate lives – and unmentioned aspects – of others? What if we dared to assume that there was – at points – greater similarity than we ever supposed?

We might then be able to conceive that, against the evidence, other people too might constantly be wracked with anxiety and are incapable of enjoying things until they are safely over; that other people too might seldom understand great works of art, pretend to have read certain great books, mouth modish political views and might frequently be thinking of their bowels and how safely to let out a fart. Other people too might do some very disgusting things with their bogeys and eat in greedy and unhygienic ways alone in the kitchen at night. Others too might have fleeting thoughts about wanting to jump onto the train tracks, lick the toilet bowl or take a tempting item from a stranger's plate in a restaurant. Others too might fantasise about seducing a relative or a colleague at work. Others too might alternate between entertaining some mean and jealous thoughts about their friends – that they might fail professionally or be abandoned in love – and wanting the best for them. They too might, beneath a polished surface, have little clue about what is going on at many moments in the office. Yet despite the darkness and the cynicism, there might be great reserves of goodness in them as well. They might be desperate to be of service, their hearts might long to reach out to others, they might be very ready to help a stranger in need.

Out of a misplaced shyness and a sharp feeling of freakishness, we trust – against the likely evidence – that there can't be too many people like us around. And yet, for better and for worse, there are in fact close to 8 billion of us waiting to be witnessed in all our strangeness, pettiness and grace, as soon as we can face up to what we already know is inside ourselves.

Our secret wish never to find love

The process of locating a partner to love is famously so hard it may for a long time disguise an alternative, even more complicated reality: that whatever we claim, it would be a lot easier for us if we never found them. The hurdles of dating undeniably exist; that doesn't mean that they aren't also being gratefully used to hide – mostly from ourselves – a harder-to-mention wish to remain on our own.

Consciously, we may tell ourselves that we would dearly love to land on a compatible soul. Inside, we are hard at work ensuring we won't – and for a variety of hugely understandable reasons:

- because it is simply too painful to hope
- because we have realised that we have too much talent for identifying characters who can torment us
- because we have had enough of other people's madness and too much experience of our own
- because humans may be best enjoyed from a distance
- because recovery from a love that promised a future robs us of too many of our remaining years
- because we have understood – finally – how properly difficult we are to live with

- because no one is as perfect or as docile as the many attractive strangers we will never speak to
- because longing alone can be so much more gratifying than a scratchy day-to-day reality together
- because if we never love, we cannot be hurt
- because there has to be a limit to how many times we can be expected to take off our clothes in front of a stranger
- because we didn't have the sort of childhood to develop the right instincts for this game

But, as these are difficult thoughts to own up to, to ourselves and our friends, we may prefer to disguise our true intentions behind a choreography of well-designed failures. Love would have been delightful, it was just that:

- We chose people who we knew would be busy.
- We failed to call back those who were keen.
- We left the party before most people arrived.
- They're all 'boring' or 'unattractive'.
- We disappointed others before they stood any chance of disappointing us.

As a result, we can continue to experience with security one of the most risk-free of all beliefs: that we would love to love, if only we found the right person ... We may be denied a partner, but we can hold on to something yet more precious: a sense of safety and a sure belief that the appropriate candidate would, if they arrived, be capable of solving our suffering. There may be few stronger romantics than those who manage carefully – and sometimes perhaps even wisely – to steer clear of anyone to be romantic with.

On fault-finding

The problem with trying accurately to identify the behaviour known as fault-finding – defined as an obsessive need to focus on the flaws and shortcomings of others – is that every human does appear to have a more or less endless and constantly irksome supply of flaws. However much we might wish it to be otherwise, human wrongness is the rule. This one has a slightly irritating laugh; that one goes on too long; this one is too insecure; that one is a bit grandiose; this one is overly practical, that one has their head in the clouds.

It can therefore take a very long time indeed to realise that what we might have on our hands – or might be ourselves – is a fault-finder, that is, someone who doesn't simply happen to discover this or that shortcoming in another person but who systematically and obsessively needs to find everyone awful as a defence against the risks of intimacy; someone with a categorical desire to conclude that everyone is not worth bothering with so that they can continue to ensure that they will never be hurt by anyone (again).

So long as everyone is defective and blemished, there can never be any need to enter into a relationship. So long as everyone is no good, there is always a sound reason to stay alone – while seeming all the while to be desperately in search of connection, which they claim has been foiled by unfortunate examples of our species.

The sad part is why the fault-finder came to be this way: because someone else, probably a parent, constantly and intolerably found fault with them. Even though children are almost universally endearing, fault-finding parents can always decide that a given child might be too quiet or bad at maths or not athletic enough or ugly from the left side. And the inevitable result of having been found fault with in this way is that we will grow up to assiduously hunt out the blemished sides of those around us (and, below the radar, of ourselves too, of course). Without a memory of a secure, properly tolerant relationship with another human, fault-finding won't just be an intellectual proclivity; it will be an emotional necessity.

What the fault-finder misses is that love doesn't involve not finding fault; it means being generous around faults. What distinguishes the fault-finder from the kindly soul isn't the number of flaws they see, it's how they interpret them. And yet we should insist that the kindly soul isn't ultimately a 'better' person – that would be to find too much fault with fault-finders. They just had the good fortune of having had a much, much easier childhood.

The promises of marriage

For many of us, there is one – and only one – way to feel truly safe in a relationship: by getting married. Once we are married, the questions will end, the doubts will cease, the dangers will ebb. We will no longer be at risk of being suddenly abandoned or randomly betrayed. We'll have the emotional security we craved for so long.

The logic is extremely powerful – and enduringly popular. But it is not, for that matter, entirely sound or beyond exploration. The link between the act of marriage and a functioning (and therefore, in the deep sense, properly secure) relationship is complex. What will ultimately shield two people is not a legal status, it's a set of emotional virtues: it's that each person feels understood, heard and seen, a condition that requires conversation, physical contact, laughter, generosity and constant acts of sacrifice and imagination. Such qualities may, of course, flourish in a marriage. But there is no necessary connection between the work that sustains love and a sternly worded piece of paper from the government.

Indeed, there can be pernicious and paradoxical ways in which the act of marriage endangers the very love it was meant to shelter. A focus on marriage can so subsume a couple – the ceremony, the cake, the guests and the gifts can become such resonant symbols of connection – that the couple end up, almost without noticing it, neglecting the emotional intimacy that their official status was intended to pay homage to. The symbol of love may get confused with love itself.

Under the sway of marriage, a couple may let go of some of the active efforts they once made to keep each other close. Feeling that a partner could not now possibly leave, they may behave in precisely the ways that would make a departure more likely. There is nothing like a nagging sense that one's partner has options to focus the mind on ensuring that they won't have any cause to deploy them.

A relationship needs to be fought for every day. That one has a piece of paper in a drawer stating that one is in a couple means

– in the end – almost nothing. A couple lives not because the government says so but because someone has remembered to say sorry; someone has, with kindness, said, 'I hear you, that must have been difficult. I'm going to try harder ...'; someone has done the washing up without being asked; someone has come up from behind and given the other a tender hug. The heart is a rebellious organ. If it's been denied its true needs, no societal decree will ever manage to quell it.

Love is like a species of delicate flower that needs continual tending. That some of these flowers have lasted thirty or forty years shouldn't mislead us; they never do so spontaneously. Marriage is only ever a seed. No elaborate ceremony nor twelve-layered cake will give a conjugal couple any substantial advantage over one that just formed a month ago in which either party can relocate to another continent at any moment without consequence.

Marriage may – of course – give some useful protection to children, and it can be an efficient way to administer property, tax and pensions, but in terms of its power to concretise emotions, its utility is ambiguous at best. Too often, it may just become an excuse not to minister to the love that inspired it. The only way for two people to attain the life-long love they might seek is for them to acknowledge that they are always free to go, that they are only ever here because they want to be, that what keeps them close is that they feel heard, seen and witnessed and that it is in their power to make – or unmake – love every new day.

The way to guarantee long-term love

A fear that a relationship we depend on could end suddenly and mysteriously can leave us yearning for techniques that could somehow help to guarantee it for the long term.

Of the many options, one stands out for being at once highly effective and distinctly counterintuitive: that two people should regularly be able (always with politeness and calm) to tell each other how frustrated they are with dimensions of their life together; how much being in their couple can, on certain occasions, be irritating, stifling, boring, even maddening; how much they might, at rare times, long to be with someone else. Far from presaging the end of love, this degree of well-handled, respectful honesty can be precisely what helps to solidify a bond for the very long term.

It may be pleasant to be around someone who allows us to tell them a stream of sweet things; it's a veritable wonder – and one that we won't want to let go of easily at all – to be around someone who allows us to tell them the truth, part of which will inevitably, after a long span together, have its complicated and challenging sides.

It's when we have been given room by our partner to mention – very gently – that there are friends of theirs we don't especially like, that there are worries they have that we don't have too much inherent sympathy for or that there are traits in their characters we wish would change, that our enthusiasm for them may grow to a pitch. It's precisely when we can admit that there is annoyance and boredom and perfidy mixed in with our tenderness and adoration, that we will be least inclined to abandon them – and will come away with a special glow of gratitude and renewed will to cement our bonds.

Though we may in some playful and brave moods ask our partners to tell us everything they're thinking, we in general do so only with a crucial, silent, incautious caveat in tow: 'But be sure not to include anything that might remotely threaten me.' Rarely do we have any advanced appetite to sample the complete range of things liable to be circulating in a partner's imagination. We stick to wanting to hear news that they like everything about us, that they've never looked at another person with desire and that they have at no point considered, for even a moment, making a life with anyone other than us.

Such thoughts may be beautiful and touching, but if this is all we have a capacity for, we will – paradoxically – be unlikely to be in a good position to build the kind of close and lasting relationship we profess to want. It's almost a precondition of a solid union that we should be able to let into circulation a degree of perplexing material that can't help but arise whenever two people grow properly close and committed.

What dividends might be repaid if we were to allow the emotional oculus to open more widely and could dare to look at some of the less unalloyed material that might be in our partner's mind (as it is in ours); if we could listen without panic as they explained that they sometimes did happen to fantasise about a stranger or dream of a new life elsewhere.

What should allow us to stay steady in the face of such revelations is the memory of our own experience. We should understand in relation to them, because we know it of ourselves, that it's entirely possible to momentarily want our partner dead and also adore them; or to be fundamentally loyal and, at times, be briefly drawn to betrayal. We'll be sanguine in the face of their news because we'll know how little our own complicated feelings have, in fact, ever been able to damage our love.

The lover around whom we'll be most comfortable, to whom we'll show the greatest loyalty and be least likely to leave, is the very person who is most willing to countenance the greatest share of our complicated, ambivalent truths.

Am I not so keen – or do I have a fear of intimacy?

If we were introducing a proverbial Martian to the ways of earthly life, one of the many somewhat dispiriting complexities we'd need to mention is that humanoids don't seem to have too much of an innate ability to understand whether they are in love or not. The greatest emotion of which we're capable is also one whose very existence we seem – with certain tragic consequences – to have a hard time discerning.

Imagine we were in a relationship in which we appreciated our partner in a host of ways but at the same time wondered – perhaps with increasing intensity – whether we should continue with them or not.

To have such doubts might indicate that we should cleanly draw the relationship to a close, but that would be to miss a painful nuance likely to nag strongly at the conscience of any moderately informed, psychologically aware person at large today: am I really not so keen or might I – deep down – simply have a fear of intimacy? Is my desire to quit evidence of disinterest or – paradoxically – proof of an interest so intense and therefore so threatening to my sense of integrity that it has triggered a wish to flee?

That we should find ourselves ruminating in this way is a legacy of pioneering work carried out across the second part of the 20th century by a cohort of psychotherapists, including John Bowlby, Erich Fromm, George Bach, David Shulman and Leslie Greenberg, who in slightly different ways all posited the theory that we humans are under the sway of two diametrically opposed inclinations: to seek closeness with others on the one hand and on the other to escape from them for fear of letdown, generally created by an actual experience of letdown during a childhood that has not been sufficiently explored or understood.

The theory places us at the sharp end of the dilemmas of self-knowledge. We might be sitting across the table from someone at dinner with a strong impression that we'd be better off with another candidate and, at the same time, outside of conscious awareness, be thinking in this way only because it was our companion's rightness that was gnawing at our walled-off, emotionally reticent and wounded characters.

How might we learn to separate out a legitimate aversion for someone from an inhibition about intimacy? We might start by asking ourselves some of the following questions:

1. Complete the sentence: *if someone knew me completely, they would think I was ...*

Some of what may lie behind our desire to get out of a relationship as it deepens is an unease about being truly known. The more someone sees who we are, the more they might take fright at what they discover. A fear of intimacy may in essence come down to a belief in our fundamental unacceptability.

2. Which of the following seems most immediately true:
   a) People can be trusted.
   b) People let you down.

We don't want to stick around, not because we dislike the partner so much as because nothing in our pasts suggests to us that people in general are capable of extensive loyalty or kindness. It isn't the partner's sweetness that is alarming us – so much as our unconscious trepidation as to when it might end, as our history suggests it always will.

3. In life in general, how easy do you find it to be happy?

Our love stories should be considered alongside our broader capacities for contentment, the extent to which we can derive pleasure from any experience, be it a holiday, a gift, money or visible success.

Being content in any way may alarm us because it might once have triggered the jealousy or sadness of an angry or fragile parent. We may find it easier to fail than to be threatened because we have won.

4. When did this desire to leave your partner set in? Did you ever feel keen – or did your coldness descend principally once they decided they felt warmly for you?

It pays to look closely at chronology – and explore whether the nauseous feeling has arisen recently or would have been there from the start. The real issue may not have anything to do with a dislike of the partner overall. We may just not be able to forgive them for one specific lapse: that they have had the bad taste to approve of someone like us. We could start to respect them once more, if only they would come to their senses and better align their view of us with our view of ourselves. The issue may be self-hatred, not hatred or disinterest per se.

5. Did your parents offer their love freely or were they – in a variety of ways – a bit of a challenge?

Adult love sits upon a base formed in childhood; and our pasts may have taught us that the really interesting, special people are those who are not generally available, don't warmly approve and always mix their affection with judgement and aloofness. The principal mistake of a current partner might be that they aren't following the script of pain we have been habituated to expect. They don't have the tricky personalities of those we grew up to admire. They are entirely alien – and therefore daunting – in their steady kindness.

*

The theory of the fear of intimacy has hugely enriched our analyses of what may be at play in love. Optimistically, it has given us a handy way of communicating a problem for which we should be understood rather than condemned. We can now explain to our partners that we have something poignant to confess: that we don't truly want to run away; we're just wrestling with a very powerful but unreliable itch to escape an unfamiliar, unwarranted feeling of being accepted. And even if we are not in the grip of this disease at all, its renown has been of help. All over the world, there are now legions of people who no longer need to believe that they have been abandoned because there was ever anything wrong with them. They were fine enough, even very much in the right. It was just that they had the misfortune to encounter another one of those well-charted scoundrels: a terrified intimacy-avoider.

Self-deception in love

We hear a lot about the problems of cheating in love, rather less about the dangers of self-deception. The cheat lies to their partner; more troublingly (for the issue is far harder to spot, let alone get cleanly incensed about), the self-deceiver is caught up in lying to themselves. They may be involved in two common pieces of emotional bad faith:

- They stay in a relationship because they are scared of being alone.

Or:

- They stay in a relationship because they are terrified of how a partner might respond to a break up.

We can say straight away that neither of these two pieces of self-deception is motivated by anything as morally stark as 'evil'; they are evasions that have more to do with a sense of weakness and underconfidence, with an acute sensitivity to causing upset and a misjudged yet still real desire for kindness. These are the holes into which some otherwise very nice people fall.

How then might we unpick these self-deceptions of which we ourselves may have been involved? The following questions might help to jog the mind to greater clarity:

1. *Can we clearly imagine someone better?*

All love involves compromise, but this truism masks that not all compromises are equally legitimate or fair. We should be with a person if, and perhaps only if, we are in a position to declare that their faults fall comfortably within the category of 'the inevitable failings of every human'. In other words, if their faults seem to us to be of the kind we could reasonably expect to have to suffer around anyone we could meet (another candidate might not be late all the time or have such an irritating best friend, but they would – perhaps – leave the bathroom in a mess or exercise too little, etc.) And yet if we suspect that the issues with our partner are on an uncommon and structurally unnecessary scale, then we owe it to ourselves – and, as importantly, to them – to acknowledge our underlying optimism about the remaining candidate pool, a hope that will otherwise pave the way for a permanent restless, secret background search for an upgrade. We should stay when we are convinced that anyone would be comparably flawed; we should leave, before more damage is done, when we feel in our bones that there can be better.

2. *Which currently feels worse for you: the idea of being alone or the idea of being with the wrong person?*

So long as the thought of being alone feels overwhelming and appalling, we are in no fit position to assess the virtues of any partner we might be with. We must be entirely reconciled with our own company to end up in the right company. The price of happy coupledom is contented singlehood. It helps to have known the particular nightmare of being with the wrong person. We need to understand intense levels of frustration and, ironically, the 'loneliness' involved in a dysfunctional couple as compared with the quiet, melancholy isolation of the single state. To make a clear choice in love, we should be able to willingly pick the dangers of being alone forever over the yet more tortuous risks of life with an incompatible partner.

3. *You are offered a newly developed tool that can magically get rid of your present partner without them needing to suffer in any way; they'll wake up and never know what happened. Do you choose to use it?*

If we are tempted to say yes, if we truly would press the button to deliver a painless blow, then we can know that what is holding us back isn't really love for our partner, it's a fear of the upset that leaving them would generate. We aren't being nice; we're terrified of the pain that another's tears would cause us. We aren't thinking about them at all; we're thinking about our wish to remain 'good' in our own eyes. There's nothing remotely wrong with deciding a person isn't for us. There is something substantially difficult with wasting another's precious time while we continue to sidestep a piece of awkward news in our own minds.

*

It might, in all this, be easier if we could believe that we're lying because we're bad; we're lying – more poignantly – because we're scared. Self-knowledge requires – on top of everything else – an unholy amount of courage.

III.

The Body

What the body wants to tell us

The most curious and hazardous feature of the way we're built lies in the difficulty we have registering a lot of what we actually feel. Our vast and strange minds get filled with unsifted thoughts and feelings we don't have the courage to look at. We might be angry or sad while lacking any active awareness that we are so, or guilty or envious without any grasp of what is at play behind a thin psychological curtain. And we remain unconscious – always – because we are resistant to ideas that threaten our sense of calm, our self-image and our gratifying illusions about ourselves. We surely can't be angry because we're kind people who couldn't feel negatively about a beloved elderly relative. Or we can't be sad at not being invited to the party because we don't care about trivial social matters. And it isn't possible that we are envious because we aren't people to covet others' advantages.

While the greatest share of our mental apparatus privileges forgetting over understanding, we do – nevertheless – have a conscience. There's a part of us that wants the truth, however bitter it might be, a minor part, but a notoriously insistent and ingenious part that won't leave us in peace until its case has been heard. It will, in order to stir us from our reverie, give us all manner of problems – breakdowns, illnesses, twitches, compulsions – in the hope of letting us know that there is something we would benefit from reckoning with.

When our conscience has done everything it can to alert our minds, it has a tendency to set to work on our bodies. More specifically, it forces us to feel in the form of a symptom what we haven't felt outright as an idea or insight. Lack of awareness returns to haunt us as physical ailments.

If our intellect won't look at our anger, the feeling may be sent to dwell in our lower back. If our anxiety isn't being dealt with psychologically, it may be relegated to our gut. Romantic frustration that is denied may – literally – begin to wreck our hearts. Our unfelt feelings end up as back pain, constipation, insomnia, migraines and arrhythmias.

However well-meaning, doctors seldom know to ask the right questions. They picture themselves fixing material problems caused by material malfunctions, not considering that it might be an ex-partner who has broken our kidney or a stifled rage against our father that is freezing up our vertebrae.

We need to do the work ourselves. In order to spare our bodies some of their mute agonies, we should submit them to a curious-sounding but strangely revealing exercise.

With our eyes closed, probably while we are lying in bed, we should gently pass over our different organs and zones and ask, if this could speak, what might it want to tell us? What might the heart ask for, the legs, the shoulders, the stomach?

Our minds are probably better able to think of answers than we presume. It could be surprisingly clear – once we ask the question – that our shoulders are desperate for the relationship to end, that our stomachs want us to take on less responsibility, that our hearts want a chance to say sorry, that our ribcage has had enough of pretending it is happy and that our lungs need an opportunity to scream.

Many of our bodily ailments are ultimately mute forms of revenge for all the thoughts and feelings we have assiduously been refusing to entertain or even acknowledge. We will feel so much better in our bodies once we have repatriated our concerns to our minds, once we have reversed the process of forgetting and dared to see and endure what we have been in flight from for too long.

The logic of sexual fantasies

Our minds seldom feel stranger than when it comes to our sexual fantasies. Otherwise sober people will find they derive erotic excitement – for reasons they probably in no way understand – from very specific items of clothing, or from words and scenarios that entirely contravene their normal orientations and commitments.

It can be tempting to dismiss these fantasies as fundamentally meaningless – refusing to endow them with anything as respectable as logic. But if we are prepared to ask the right questions of them, they may shed considerable light on themes in our lives; they may hold the clue to central, challenging aspects of our biographies.

The clue to unlocking their meaning is to consider sexual fantasies as attempts to master, and gain some form of victory over, difficult incidents or dynamics; to see them, in essence, as an eroticisation of pain. The sexual act, standing outside the demands and strictures of ordinary existence, emerges as a minor and redemptive utopian moment in which we strive – either in our imaginations or in the presence of companions – to put right some of what went wrong in the world beyond.

Let's imagine a person who, in their daily routines, carries a huge degree of responsibility: perhaps they stand at the head of a busy family, team or corporation. Maybe they have, since their earliest days and not necessarily as the result of any free choice, fallen into the role of the sensible one to whom people will look to for direction (they may have been the eldest sibling, or a parent might have been ill or have absconded). Then imagine that this person, in their sexual imagination, experiences a longing to submit entirely to the will of someone else. In bed, they strictly don't want to be in charge. Here they want another person to tell them sternly what to do; here the authority that they normally possess is willingly thrown aside in the name of trusting passivity and meek compliance. Rather than giving orders, they thrill to receive them; rather than the burden of being important, they revel in a sense of their insignificance.

It can all sound hugely peculiar – but interpreted as an attempt to rectify the excessive or painful circumstances of non-erotic life, it starts to make sense. The sexually submissive person is – for a privileged period of time – seeking a way out of an arduous degree of power and responsibility.

Or, to look at an opposed but related pattern, imagine someone who, in daily life, always displays a heightened timidity. Maybe, as a child, there was a threatening parent who could not countenance signs of assertion or aggression. Now they show only reticence, extreme politeness and modesty, a degree of self-abnegation that may be exhausting to their spirit, which is why there may be such intense pleasure, in sex, in becoming someone else: a person who can, at last, in a safe way, with the full consent of an experienced adult, give vent to an untrammelled power and raw belligerence. Here – like nowhere else – they can boss someone around, tell them what to do, brook no excuses, explore their ruthless, cruel sides – and recover contact with aspects of their personality that have been unfairly denied to them in their development.

We can, as we survey our own fantasies, ask ourselves one central question: in what way might this desire constitute an eroticisation of pain? What might the pain have been? And how does the fantasy signify an attempt to overcome a source of prior discomfort or suffering?

All scenarios, even the less well-known ones, are likely to reveal logic through this lens. Imagine, for example, someone who likes to watch their partner being seduced by a third person. One might hazard that behind this fetish there lies the experience of having been painfully excluded by someone one depended on. Inviting in a third person constitutes an attempt to gain a victory over marginalisation.

Or imagine someone extremely drawn to the idea of a busy and rather stern professional person in uniform – a pilot, a firefighter, a doctor – who promptly throws aside their diligence in the name of liberated sex. The pain here might be related to a feeling of not mattering enough to an impressive but aloof caregiver.

Or imagine someone drawn to the scenario of a very reserved, prudish person – they might be employed in a library or a monastery or a nunnery – discarding their reticence in the name of sexual abandon. Here, similarly, there might have been a figure in the past who seemed painfully frightened of sex and cut off from its liberating power. Enacting a scenario of pleasure among the bookshelves constitutes a victory over a sexual dysfunction which one unconsciously observed with regret.

It's easy to feel perturbed and even scared by some of the oddities of our desires. By viewing them as nothing more or less than attempts to eroticise difficulties in the past, we emerge as more interesting and sensible to ourselves and better able to explain who we are to those we care about.

The logic of dreams

We are rarely as odd – or as impenetrable – to ourselves as when we dream. Minds, over which we have a reasonable measure of jurisdiction during daylight hours, become entirely peculiar to us as we slip our conscious moorings. It is as if an extremely unconventional film director were nightly to seize control of our inner projection screen and involve us in a succession of intricate adventures and dilemmas before leaving us frightened and bewildered on the shores of dawn. They might take us to Spain but recreate a street so that it looks like Chicago; they might hire a former colleague for the role of an astronaut; they might take over the family home of the first person we went out with and insert a swimming pool in the bathroom; they might summon a long-dead grandmother back to life to be the passenger in a taxi we're driving. More confusingly still, this tricksy film director must be us, but not a version of us that in any way tallies with what we know of ourselves.

One method for trying to make sense of dreams is to imagine that, during the night, the mind operates under a very strict rule: it needs to think about its central preoccupations, to process the troubles and excitements of the day, but it can only do so indirectly, by turning them into abstract, metaphoric versions of themselves. Nothing can show up in a dream as it actually is in waking life. There can't be straightforward references to emotions like guilt or sorrow – nor to events like a separation or an argument. The rules of the night are akin to a game in which we can speak only using words other than the ones we normally deploy; for example, being given the sentence 'The man walked into the room' and having to remake it so that it reads: 'The animal that has no tail nor fur advanced with scissor-like motions into a giant cube the size of a car pointed upwards.'

What makes this constant transposition necessary is a requirement not to get too close to difficult emotional material that might wake up the dreamer. The dream constitutes a compromise position between a desire to explore a challenging emotional truth on the one hand – and to stay asleep, on the other. Too much truth and one would wake up. Too much distance from live material and one wouldn't be able to process the material as necessary. We can think of the mind as a spy operating behind enemy lines who is able to communicate with its base only using a secret language – made up of pictures and symbols – which won't be understood by the authorities.

Let's imagine someone who needs to process a sense of anger with their mother, who then dreams – according to the rules of the game – about visiting a live volcano in the presence of an unusually tall hen. Or someone oppressed by the touching but burdensome loyalty of their partner having a dream about a large, friendly dog returning repeatedly to them with a bone that hardly fits inside their room.

We can picture the mind facing an implicit challenge every night: deal with the emotions that have to be explored but do so without mentioning any of the literal characters or settings involved. You will need to think about your son and his career dilemma, but you can't mention either your son or the dilemma. Or you need to think about your rocky marriage but without directly referencing either your spouse or your troubles. It's a major artistic challenge every time – but our minds are more than up to the task. The idea of claiming to lack an imagination makes – from this perspective – no sense at all.

Knowing the rules of the game, when we wake up and our dream is still fresh, before we open the curtains or get up, we might continue to lie in bed and write down a dream's key moments. We should keep in mind that the dream is a metaphor or transposition of something very close to home and try to decode what is at play: what could a speedboat travelling through a swamp be an allusion to? Who might an authoritarian innkeeper be? What might a mountain coated with snow that is also chocolate represent?

However puzzling our nighttime visions might be, they are not nonsense signifying nothing. They are narratives full of intentions that need to be known, yet that one part of the mind, in the name of a good night's rest, doesn't cleanly want to communicate with the other. Once we have secured our sleep, we can afford to go back and unravel the code; we can undo the work of the genius-level film director in the name of a closer and less frenetic appreciation of our real concerns.

What it isn't in the power of the mind to fix

We are large-brained creatures with strong tendencies to assume that most of our problems have been caused by our minds and must, therefore, through intense focus, be fixed by our minds. When feelings of sadness or confusion descend, we typically try to fire up our frontal lobes and address our pains by heroically striving to think ourselves out of them. We draw up lists, we write a journal, we seek out a friend or a therapist, we might look up a book of psychology or philosophy.

There may be much benefit, but there is also – occasionally – more wisdom still in realising the limits of reason. Not every problem that manifests in the mind was created in the mind – or can, for that matter, be solved by the mind, however assiduously and energetically it proceeds. Parents of young children come to know this lesson particularly well. There can be moments when a small person's mood sinks dramatically and constellations of negative ideas start to grip themselves very tightly around the juvenile mind: another child has a better toy and it's outrageous; it's a tragedy that a favourite film isn't on television; the dinner is completely disgusting; the button on a beloved jacket is coming off and will never be fixed ... The temptation can be to try to reason with the young person, to dig them out of their perplexed state through the use of ideas (the button can be mended, perhaps; the film that's on now – while not perhaps as exciting as the one last week, nevertheless ...). But an experienced parent suspects that the real cause of the distemper may lie elsewhere entirely: the child is just exhausted and needs to go to bed immediately. These catastrophic forebodings aren't conclusions carefully reached through reason; they're emanations of an affliction which only a nap can answer.

For all our later sophistication, adults too frequently wind up in the same position. We too might decide that life has no inherent purpose, that our friends are profoundly ungrateful, that our work has no sense and that everyone is out to get us, but if we knew ourselves better, we would perceive that, like frantic toddlers, we simply need to get to bed quickly or should urgently pour ourselves a large glass of orange juice. Existential anxiety may, in the end, be mostly a matter of low blood sugar. To know ourselves properly is to learn to separate out a problem that manifests in the mind from one that is caused by the mind.

Even in cases where a problem truly does seem to be a mental one, it isn't always by sitting down and attempting to reason our way out of it via a frontal cognitive assault that we can come to the best results. There are knots in thinking that are best unravelled by ceasing to think entirely, by pushing our chair aside and taking off for a walk around the block, listening to a song or taking in an undemanding film.

The mind may be doing its best work precisely when we don't ask too much of it too urgently. It may be when we are ostensibly not doing anything much – gazing out of the window, studying the way a branch tapers down to the earth or watching a squirrel make its way impishly up the trunk – that important ideas can loosen themselves from the grip of our agitated, over-hasty enquiries and flower properly. We may be doing some of our best thinking while following the horizon on a long train journey, or watching our toes in the course of a long hot bath. We may need to reduce an inhibiting sense of the importance of what we're doing in order to do it properly – and so might need to take ourselves out to a forest that was already mature before Columbus set sail, or admire Polaris, 433 light years away, on a clear, moonlit walk. We can return to ourselves readier to contribute when we have been reminded of our negligible place in the greater whole.

We have no sensible option but to work in sync with the unconscious, ceding to it when we have done our best in the rational cockpit, gracefully giving way to its more mysterious, slow-moving and elusive workings. Just as someone inside us decides how to digest lunch or put one foot in front of the other without the conscious self ever being consulted, so too may ideas be forming without us needing to be 'there' to deliver them. Indeed, they may gestate in far more original and beautiful ways if we take our leave for a time or spend an hour gardening or entertaining a dog instead of forcing them to obey a timetable set by an office or a teacher. We must, like skilful sailors, adjust our sails to mysterious prevailing inner winds.

There is naturally something humiliating in how little control we can exert: our sense of who we are and what we want may be absurdly affected by what we had for dinner or how much oxygen there is in a room. But we should not compound our subjection by imagining that we can ever escape it. To think well is to respect all that thinking alone cannot directly achieve.

IV.

Society

The sinner inside us all

In the public squares of the cities of Northern Europe in the Middle Ages, to see a person 'in stocks', their arms, head and legs immobilised within a wooden frame, was a standard sight. The person (it was more often than not a woman) had done something wrong – they'd committed adultery, they'd not gone to church enough, they'd read a suspicious book, they'd danced too much, they'd communicated with satanic spirits – and their punishment was to be laughed at, doused in urine or have excrement and offal thrown at them. We shudder at how uncivilised we once were.

Yet we have not, of course, entirely given up on stocks. We too have our range of media-identified villains and our versions of verbal offal: this one slept with the wrong person, that one was privately recorded saying something inappropriate, this other one accepted money from a dubious source. And so, we'll get to work on insults and calumny. Often – as in the Middle Ages – the way we justify our brutality is with reference to our enemy's degraded nature; we can be severe because they have been impure.

Our high-handed cruelty is so regrettable in part because it contravenes the laws of self-awareness. The more we understand of ourselves, the more we necessarily reach a surprising, humbling realisation: most of what we condemn in other people is present in ourselves. There is a reprobate, a weirdo, a pervert, a freak, a glutton and a bigot in all of us. The more incensed we are of the 'sin' in another, the more we are likely to be harbouring a version of it in our own characters. The strength of our condemnation only indicates how deeply involved we are in matters like impiety, lust, selfishness, tribalism, greed and retrogression. We rush to condemn the wicked out of an unprocessed relationship with our own impurity.

Maturity demands something far more challenging: that we accept without righteousness the presence in our minds of all kinds of impulses and thoughts that violate prevailing morals. We too – like the unfortunate characters in stocks who we have enjoyed laughing at – have had wicked thoughts and perhaps done wicked deeds. We are infinitely complicated creatures, drawn to the light but ineluctably caught up in the darkness, prone to temptation, aspiring to nobility yet repeatedly drawn to baseness.

What should replace offal-throwing is a weary, compassionate sadness for our whole race. The person in stocks is not uniquely sinful; they are perhaps merely uniquely unlucky. Impulses that dwell in all of us were given untrammelled opportunities in their case; we might have acted likewise if we had had their path through life. We should – with self-awareness – shudder for ourselves and pity those who have erred.

We will have grown up when we can bear to recognise that every flaw we curse in people around us is nascent in our minds. Self-exploration should provide the definitive cure for feelings of superiority. To rehearse a by-now familiar point (with a tragically weak hold on our minds), we'll be kind to others when we can bear to acknowledge the sinful parts of ourselves.

The historical causes of modern unhappiness

When trying to understand why we might be feeling unhappy, we tend to be drawn to reasons relatively close to home: we might zero in on issues to do with friends, relationships, health, jobs, families or schedules. What we tend not to do, however, is start talking about our place in history; it would sound overblown or plain bizarre to begin to pin a sizeable share of our difficulties on broad historical and sociological forces. It's our personal failings and intimate dilemmas that we principally look to in order to explain our weary or troubled spirits.

Yet whatever role our psyches and our families and colleagues might be playing in our moods, a proper understanding of our situation cannot be complete without consideration of the highly peculiar and novel era in which we exist. We are troubled in part because we dwell in highly unbalanced times:

Transcendence

At the centre of all premodern societies were powers that helped to put humans in their place: older, bigger, stronger, holier phenomena, perhaps a god, a natural energy or a spirit. However important humans might have felt, however grand the aristocracy or urgent the news of the day, people knew that they were not the measure of all things, that above and beyond the earthly realm there was something else – more mysterious, imposing and strange – to which they would all regularly have to bow, and which would relativise them in one another's eyes. The fanciest king was nothing next to a thunderous god, the mightiest invention pathetic next to an angry sea.

But we humans are now the most astonishing things we can conceive of: it's our momentous doings, our intelligence, our incomprehensibly wondrous technologies that mesmerise us and are at the centre of collective consciousness. For many of us, God has died and nature is to be pitied and patronised like a wounded, once-proud animal. We have lost any redeeming sense of our own unimportance.

Expectations

We are, at the same time – each one of us – told repeatedly that we could do and be anything. We might – with sufficient hard work – assume the presidency, unlock a major scientific secret or become known to the entire planet through our athletic or artistic prowess. We are also thereby subtly informed that only a very special destiny is valid. There is no dignity left in a so-called ordinary life; there can be nothing to celebrate in an unheralded, unknown existence. We cannot live quietly and be in bed by nine. We must become someone – or else look on with envy and rage at those who have evaded the perils of mediocrity.

Media

We used to know almost nothing of what happened beyond our own valley or shoreline. Life went by so slowly that we were often – without appreciating how much this kept us sane – a little bored. Now no bloodshed, scandal, upset or peril can occur anywhere on the planet without us hearing of it in minutes – and we are, as a result, in a state of continuous unrest and alarm, unable to set anything negative in context, unsure of how to evaluate our species, terrified to trust or speak to a stranger, constantly feeling that we are leading the wrong lives. We know everything – except the less perceptible things that really matter. Our attention is drawn only to our discords, our spitefulness and our cruelty. We have been stripped of opportunities to contemplate older, slower currents, to draw inspiration from the dawn, the murmurings of doves or robins or the barks of ancient trees that speak of time measured in centuries.

Isolation

We have been sold the idea that the one solution to our loneliness lies in romantic love. We therefore search with frantic abandon in the lonely concrete canyons of our modern megalopolises for one very special being who can be everything to us: best friend, sexual partner, playmate, kindergarten teacher, cook, chauffeur, etc. And then when (inevitably) we cannot find them, we perceive ourselves as having been uniquely cursed. We misunderstand the generality of the problem – and miss the solace available in the less febrile and prestigious realm of friendship, in distributing our needs more equitably among a whole community, none of whose members need to answer to the whole of anyone's longings. We've been rendered exceptionally lonely by the unwittingly cruel notion of a soulmate.

Work

We could – back then – stand away from our work and see something substantial and solid that we had made: a chair, some horseshoes, a house. We now occupy ourselves with tasks that have been infinitely subdivided and which, thereby, have lost much of their wider logic. We carry professional titles like logistics controller, automation specialist or human resource manager that show us up as minute cogs in endlessly complicated engines. We may be richer than ever, but we struggle to see what difference we could possibly make to anyone else's life.

Self-discipline

All the while, we lose ourselves in temptations which our evolutionary past leaves us defenceless against. Because we were programmed to eat any sugary thing – a rare blackberry or apricot – that came our way, we now cannot resist the plethora of satanic confections on offer on every street corner. Because in our old villages we might have seen one or two attractive people a day, we now can't stop looking at ceaseless digital processions of the unclothed. We have no willpower to resist the pitiless delights of the modern world.

It is hard to reverse any of the pressures we have been placed under. But even if we cannot, knowing that these exist helps us to locate with greater fairness the origins of many of our troubles. We are not uniquely or personally awful, frantic, greedy or degenerate. We are under historically exceptional pressures. To know ourselves properly is to honour how much of our madness does not belong simply to us.

The drive to fail

We are likely to be familiar enough by now with the bare bones of an archetypal, oft-repeated story: a highly lauded and beloved person – it might be a popular politician or a famous newsreader or an actor or an athlete – is suddenly discovered to have done something hugely shocking, perhaps illegal and wholly contrary to their persona. They took drugs, they told a lie, they had an affair, they were found in a motel near the airport with a prostitute, they shouted at a colleague inappropriately off camera. And now everyone is up in arms; no one can believe what's happened. The media are in uproar, fans are in shock. Another formerly adored figure becomes a byword for scandal and transgression.

Onlookers are prone to casually describe such situations as tragedies – and to put what's happened down to a piece of almost random bad luck. But if we look at matters more psychologically, the stories rarely do emerge as accidents; a clear pattern of paradoxical but genuine intentionality seems at play. The actor or politician or newsreader didn't haphazardly end up blowing up their career. However odd it sounds, they wanted – or even, one might say – needed to do so.

Success is only endurable if it can feel – at some level – deserved, if the acclaim of the crowd and the respect of peers tally with an inner sense of worth, if we feel that by rising to a certain eminence, we are accruing our due. But there are many of us who both want to succeed and cannot bear the unreality and impudence of having done so. We begin by needing success because we are nagged inside by an appalling feeling of worthlessness, because we are in flight from a sense of shame and dishonour generated through – most often – episodes of intense cruelty, neglect and humiliation in childhood. It's rare to want to become a somebody without long, early lacerating experience of having been a nobody.

But then attaining success tends to prove hugely conflictual and troubling. At one level, it's the realisation of a dream; at another, it brings us perilously close to realising the trauma upon which our drive to triumph has been founded. At last, we have a chance to feel less persecuted and hounded by our inner critics; but the disjuncture between the outer acclaim and the inner shame is at risk of proving psychically insufferable. We seek to blow up our careers not because we don't want them but because powerful forces in our past leave us certain we don't deserve them.

The scandal or mishap that we carefully engineer represents our troubled mind's desperate attempt to return us to an inner sense of equilibrium, to make us less estranged from ourselves, to render us more loyal to feelings of disgrace which feel – despite our protests – like our true home.

We don't need to be major stars to share in this psychology. Any of us, even in more modest roles, might find success atrocious and therefore be unable to prevent ourselves from seeking outside sources of persecution to match and attenuate feelings of persecution inside. We can feel too much like criminals not to stop ourselves from seeking a crime to bring our corruption or 'sin' into focus.

It may look to outsiders that we have done something 'silly' when we steal or get caught in a damaging rumour, but what we are essentially doing is finding a way to be less happy with ourselves. In one of the most peculiar phenomena of psychology, we are out to commit a crime in order to feel better, so that we can finally know why we are 'bad' – given that the real causes of our sense of unacceptability and corruption are hidden from us.

The secret – which few celebrities realise before the press is at the door – is to become clearer about where our feeling of malignity comes from, to try as far as possible to know why we have come to distrust ourselves and why failure therefore seems the most honest albeit awful fate for us. We'll be able to withstand the burdens of success when we can better accept that we were never really bad – we were simply treated very badly.

Who would you want to bully?

It can sound odd indeed to be asked who would you want to bully. We, of course, despise the thought of bullying anyone; we are civilised members of an advanced society. It isn't our game to make others miserable – and we know the consequences if we've ever tried.

But this ethical stance – though admirable in a practical sense – is here neither helpful nor a route to insight. We aren't trying to work out who we are truly going to harm; we're trying to understand ourselves better. We want to look with rare honesty at who we would be drawn to bullying in our deep self, in the unconscious, if civilisation broke down, if we were not as controlled and mature as we strive to be – in order to grasp some of what is most fearful and confused inside us.

We might hazard a generalisation: we want to bully people who exhibit the very weaknesses – it might be shyness, helplessness, timidity or lack of authority – that we know well from within ourselves and that we probably had to pay a high price for manifesting in our early years. We want to bully a disavowed version of our younger, weaker, more naive and less controlled selves.

The bullying urge twitches ever so slightly when we catch a glimpse of a small, fussy, quiet child, a meek junior at work, a clumsy friend of a friend. Somewhere in the recesses of our minds, we are appalled; we want to expunge their errors as we had to expunge ours (under duress). Freed from all restrictions, we might want to call them a cry-baby and a weirdo and throw their belongings out of the window and get other people to join us in laughing at them – our cruelty motivated by a demented desire to prompt the weakling to reform themselves.

Something else can inflame the wish to bully: when we notice that the person with our former flaw is being treated with far greater tolerance and generosity than we were shown. Not only do we see them tainted by our weaknesses but we also enviously notice that they are getting away with their delicate behaviour. We, somewhere deep within, long to avenge ourselves of those pampered, privileged neophytes who unjustly retain an innocence so violently torn away from us.

The bullying impulse may reach an ominous pitch with one person in particular: our own child. Becoming a parent means seeing at close range someone who is very like us, who might look and sound exactly as we did – and who will naturally exhibit many of our former incapacities and infirmities. It takes considerable emotional strength not to bully as we were bullied, not to torment another for a vulnerability that was formerly derided in us; to allow our child to have a better start than we did.

Thinking something is very different from setting out to do it. Indeed, noticing a 'bad' thought is precisely what can encourage us to stiffen our ethical guardrails. It's when we can acknowledge our capacity for unpleasantness that we are motivated to make extra efforts to be benevolent. We will finally vanquish the bullying impulse when we can offer our psyches what they should have been given from the start: an experience of patience and tenderness towards their most unconfident and terrified parts.

The game of secrets

There's a game that can be played with any large group of strangers, ideally in some kind of hall, where everyone is given a pen and a sheet of paper and asked to write down – in total anonymity – the bare bones of a truly significant secret – not a cute bit of obfuscation but rather the sort of thing that might make one want to die if it was discovered – and then to fold up the sheet very tightly and drop it into a large central box. A host then reads out a selection to the group – which, to rely on some real-life examples, might include entries like:

- *I am attracted to my sister-in-law.*
- *I've married the wrong person.*
- *I want to kill myself.*
- *I don't like my eldest child.*
- *I am a porn addict.*
- *I masturbate at work.*
- *I am having an affair.*

We might, in response to such disclosures, be tempted to sigh at the complexities of human nature: all that is unconventional, dark, deceitful and uncanny about us. But there is also an option, more redemptive, to feel extremely relieved. Despite all our fears, it seems we are – in the end – not as isolated as we might have feared. We may not have precisely those secrets, but we will almost certainly have others of comparable peculiarity – that might now seem less oppressively aberrant. We are 'normal' not so much on the basis of our outwardly respectable behaviour but because we, like everyone else, cannot manage to subscribe to the prevailing orthodoxy. Anyone we meet will not be as their outward behaviour suggests; beneath a mannered surface, they – like us – will be profoundly beset by compulsions, will be going half out of their minds with alarm, will be battling cravings, will feel terror and shame at certain things they've done and will, in some moods, long never to have been born. The only people we can ever think of as 'normal' are those we don't yet know very well.

Through a game of secrets, we become familiar with what otherwise only priests and psychotherapists know: the extent to which folly is the general rule and the ferocious skill with which we manage to pretend otherwise. We could never know, scanning a room filled with an average group of our fellow citizens, that we might be in the presence of thefts, addictions, maladies and pathologies. We look so ordinary – and indeed we are. We just need to expand our notion of ordinariness to encompass the true perplexing, formidable, frightening and (from some angles at least) infinitely touching reality of human nature.

V.

Existence

Why we might refuse happiness

Happiness sounds like such an obviously desirable quality, the idea that a person might willingly turn it down makes – on the surface at least – no sense at all. Why would anyone deny themselves life's supreme end, the goal to which everything else points, the natural objective of all our endeavours?

Yet faced with the possibility of contentment, many of us do appear to manifest a curious preference for despondency. Whatever the opportunities for fulfilment, we stay distinctly loyal to caution, suspicion and fear.

We might identify six reasons why – in the end – happiness may simply prove too much of a burden to bear:

1. The association between worry and safety

We may refuse happiness because we were once hugely innocent and paid a high price for our credulity. When we were vulnerable and naive, when we could not muster strength for a fight, a blow came to us out of the darkness whose pain and surprise reverberates to this day. The relationship between being terrified and being safe now seems ironclad. It is only by being permanently primed for attack, ceaselessly on the lookout for enemies, aggressively alert to any signs of danger, that we feel we can be protected from further unwelcome surprises. The price of safety is continual circumspection.

This stance is hard to shake off because the hypervigilant person is typically unconsciously and unfairly generalising outwards from a particular traumatic incident that they have not fully remembered or engaged with. Everything feels excessively dangerous when the exact things that were once unsettling have not been maturely understood. We remain constantly with our knife at the ready because the singular injustice and malice that once befell us has proved too painful to explore.

2. *A fear of angering the gods*

For most of our time on the planet, humans have operated with a background sense of a connection between embracing happiness and angering someone – a divine figure like Zeus, Thor, Kali or Coyote – who wouldn't appreciate a mere human usurping their place at the summit of contentment.

We may no longer believe in gods, but we are liable, still dimly, to associate triumph with risk – though for reasons rather closer to home. There are fragile, unhappy parents who – despite their stated interests in their children's well-being – cannot in reality bear to see them win, are unendurably threatened by their victories and thereby bring out in them a desire to make loyal offerings of failure, to sacrifice their potential on the altar of their parents' insecurities; to privilege closeness to them over an exploration of their own talents. There are parents who leave their children no way out of an asphyxiating dichotomy: succeed or stay close to me; win the world or keep me.

No surprise then that some of us choose to mess up important exams, decide (against the evidence of the mirror) that we are ugly, become impotent or fail to flourish in line with our possibilities. No wonder that we might unconsciously opt for misery when the price of happiness seems to be to lose the love of those who placed us on the earth.

3. *A fear of excess*

One of the lessons that all good parents teach their children is how to come down safely from the heights of excitement: how to descend from jubilation to serenity. At the birthday party or the trampoline session, the good parent watches a head of euphoric steam build up and then looks out for ways in which it can be safely and gradually dissipated. Warnings are given, sympathetic but definitive rules are proposed, boundaries are enforced.

The child may kick against the limits, but they welcome them too; in the end, it's no fun to be allowed to do whatever one pleases. In time, the child learns to turn the faucet of jubilation on and off by themselves and so grows unfrightened of their own exuberance, knowing it won't threaten the return of levelheadedness and sobriety.

But offspring without such an induction may enter adulthood with greater doubts: unsure of how to be pleased with themselves without becoming permanently egomaniacal, how to feel potent without turning monstrous, how to be proud of their accomplishments without boasting. And because they can't imagine a way down, they may prefer never to look for a way up. They grow meek because – beneath a quiet, asexual, timid exterior – they can't picture how to be happy without succumbing to hubris.

4. *A terror of hope*

As prisoners attest, the real enemy of endurance is hope. If a promise of early release were to appear and then – somehow –

vanish, the return to the cell would be close to impossible to bear. A letdown is infinitely harder than static misery. We can (almost) take a death sentence; what is properly unthinkable is a violated reprieve, which is why we may tell the suitor that we cannot make dinner, the investor that we have no interest in their money or the prospective friend that we don't play tennis; we want what they offer too much to ever risk ever having to rebuild our lives if it were denied to us. We prefer the protection of sadness to the agony of aspiration.

5. *A sense of unworthiness*

A precondition of being able to enjoy the world outside us is a sense that we are deserving people inside. For some of us lacking the right sort of early experiences, happiness can feel as unmerited as it is alien. Were it to knock at our door too insistently, we might have to get tougher on its impudence. We might actively have to turn away a kind lover, we will guarantee that a long-awaited holiday won't be peaceful, we might have to take assiduous steps to blow up a friendship, we might need to make actively certain that our colleagues won't continue to respect us. Some people might call it self-sabotage. From the inside, it just feels like a sensible way to make sure we won't have to be taunted any further by opportunities we don't feel we deserve.

6. A fear of regret

We may continue to be miserable as an alternative to acknowledging that we have suffered more or less needlessly for most of our lives because it is too galling to accept that we might have squandered our best years in avoidable neuroses. We declare happiness silly in order to defend ourselves against a yet more terrifying notion: that it's our decades-long gloom that has been daft and unwarranted. We might, to make our misery seem more necessary, lean on the romantic idea of a link between sadness and depth – and happiness and superficiality. We might imply that we are too profound to laugh, that we are too clever and sensitive for joy. But we would only be doing so to run away from an infinitely more challenging idea: that to know how to giggle like a child may be one of the most serious accomplishments of any adult life.

The necessity of denial

We are primed to think well of people who have an appetite for truth: who want to find out everything they can about themselves, the world and the purpose of existence. And we may be accordingly suspicious of those flighty souls who cannot sit still with their own thoughts and who must manically escape into varied forms of distraction and denial.

Yet when we have paid due homage to the search for truth and applauded those who want to look at existence with their eyes wide open, something tricky is likely to force its way into our expectant minds. It may not – it seems – be truly possible to take on board the full fundamentals of life, the unvarnished contract at the heart of our presence on the planet, and not want to give up. Whatever our enlightenment faith in the power of knowledge, there appears to be an awkward yet inviolable relationship between remaining alive and not looking at many things too closely. Selective denial may just be the price we have to pay for enduring.

It seems unlikely, for example, that any of us can really face, at anything other than a highly abstract level, the thought that at some point in the never-too-distant future, we – with all our plans, our sensitivity, our ideas, our complex problems, the issues with our hair, our favourite recipes, our tangled relations with our parents, our nicknames from childhood, the small pain in our left knee and our tender and hopeful natures – will be wiped out, and everything we are and have ever been will grow as dim and meaningless as the lives of the 100 billion or so other humans who have come before us and whose destinies and concerns are as dust to us.

It seems equally impossible that our hugely important societies that are presently working their way through momentous political events, that are pioneering new and more just ways of living, that are caught up in varied scandals and obsessions, that are on the cusp of discovering life-altering machines, will in time – as the sun's diminishing supply of hydrogen burns up the raging oceans – end up every bit as obscure as those of the Minoans, the Khmers, the Olmecs and the Anasazis; that the beautiful and powerful of our evanescent age will eventually be as faceless as the stars of the Aksumite Empire and the leaders of the Kingdom of Funan, a confident polity that dominated mainland Southeast Asia from the 1st to the 6th centuries CE.

And were we to fall for the touching and sublime dream that it might perhaps be love that could save us and help us endure, that eternal meaning might be found in the care and concern we have for one another, then we would be wise not to look deeply into our own hearts or those of anyone else whose attentions we think would be capable of holding back the entropic forces of the universe. With poignant optimism, we might imagine, despite increasing evidence to the contrary, that it must simply be a piece of temporary bad luck that we have not yet found the love we crave, as we set out on yet another date or session with a marriage therapist. It would be as cruel to kill hope here as it would be to violently shake from their chimerical reveries a fervent believer lying prostrate on the ground in an ancient temple, mumbling obscure prayers to an empty sky for the return of a divine figure who never lived.

We have perhaps overdone the case for the truth. We are still here – and taking our plans for the day seriously – because we are, somewhere inside us, clinging tightly to a raft of necessary fictions: that things could matter, that there might be a point in speaking, that anyone can understand. The only people who have properly looked life in the face are no longer here. Insofar as we're interested in living, we have no option but to lean heavily on our powers of denial.

We should want the light of truth to shine very brightly – just never so brightly as to blind us.

Living consciously

We want – almost all of us – to live as long as possible, but in our urgent and never-guaranteed search to extend life, we ignore a more realistic and significant possibility: that of altering how intensely we live it.

Crucially, not all time is equal. Time stretches and extends the more we take hold of events, dissect them and turn them over in our minds – just as it seems to shrink and run through us when we only squint at reality, perhaps because we are too scared of the future, sad about the past, obedient to an agenda set by people around us or ambitious about what's to come.

Every minute we are alive is equal from a purely physiological basis, but at the level of the psyche, we can speak of periods of being more or less aware of being here; we can – as it were – live more or less consciously.

Without trying, small children are masters of conscious living – which is why a walk with them to the park may take four times as long as we had anticipated. There are, after all, so many leaves to examine; so many large, flat pebbles; so many walls to run one's fingers along; and concrete ledges and lines of putty to caress or palpate.

If time seems to speed up as we get older, it's because we unconsciously decide that we have, in most areas, already noticed everything that it would be significant and charming to see. We walk to the park – and around the globe – with a blindfold. Our days get emptier because we perceive ever less in them. There is no need to look too closely at trees any more, or the cables by the television, or the legs of a giraffe, or our partner's hands, or the cloud formations in mid-afternoon. It might have been three decades at least since we looked properly at an apple or a light switch. Matters that would have detained us at the age of 4 lose all definition until we discover, with horror, that it is autumn again and we don't know where another year has gone.

The difference between living and living consciously is like the difference between swallowing something at once and chewing it at length. The conscious liver doesn't merely want to have an experience; they want to work out how it operates and achieves its effect on the mind – and this in the case of two kinds of experiences in particular: painful and beautiful ones.

For example, the conscious liver might find themselves by a lake on a warm summer's day. They are – like everyone else – aware of beauty. But they also have an unusually powerful wish not to let this beauty slip away from them and seek to arrest its dispersal through a set of questions. As they look around, they might wonder: why is this moving me so much? What have I been missing throughout winter? What am I normally afraid of? How is today reassuring me? What makes this shade of blue in the sky so welcoming? What is it about the trees that makes them so enticing?

We don't need to be poets or artists to digest our experiences more thoroughly, but we can learn from these disciplines about how to study the world and bottle and preserve its most valuable moments (so that the grass and the smell of foxgloves and the sound of a song thrush will still be alive in us in early February).

We can live more consciously too around painful events. Here, as well, we can try to slow time's dispersal with a web of questions: what made that colleague so unpleasant? Why exactly are we feeling so downhearted with our friend? What lies behind our fear of people who like us too intensely? Why do we get so irritated by cynicism? Where is this present sadness about work rooted?

Once we master the art of conscious living, we can afford to be a little less concerned with how long our lives will be. Another decade more or less won't have to be the decisive matter when it lies permanently in our power to densify time, and when we can find the amount of content more normally associated with a month in the bounds of a single day. We can slow the reductive march of the clock with the tendrils of our own sensitivity.

We should perhaps stop asking how old people are and focus on a more telling and more accurate measure of their time on earth: how consciously they are living.

The always unfinished business of self-knowledge

Whatever our commitment to self-knowledge, we have no alternative but to go to our deaths having understood only a fraction of who we have been. We are – each one of us – fated to be laid to rest in an at-least-partially unknown grave.

We may – for example – never understand why certain things made us so anxious, what drove some of our behaviour in relationships or what our true working talents were. We still won't know entirely why a marriage broke up, a friendship ended in acrimony or an enthusiasm was formed. We'll burst into tears at moments we didn't expect or grow irritable or joyful without knowledge of the real sources of our anger or delight.

We can't be held entirely responsible for our ignorance. There are almost as many neurons in our brains as there are stars in the Milky Way – around 86 billion – each one capable of connecting with the others in wholly unique and hard-to-trace ways. It should be no wonder if we manage only a few fleeting sorties around certain spiral arms and superclusters. If life is like a large book, we will be interrupted no further in than one of the early chapters, our finger holding our place mid-paragraph as we breathe our last.

We can at least strive to put ourselves in situations where we stand the highest chance of meeting with the occasional insight. We might:

- lie in bed for a long time thinking
- soak in very hot baths
- take train journeys in empty carriages across open distances
- walk with curious friends
- have therapy
- read a lot
- stare out of the window at the clouds and the rain
- do so-called 'nothing' very often
- journal
- eat alone
- listen to feedback from partners, especially the difficult parts
- unpack our anxiety, sorrow, joy and anger
- look into the mirrors that colleagues, parents, children and strangers hold up to us

Throughout, we might be looking out for answers to some of the following puzzles:

- how our childhoods have shaped us
- what we project
- what we deny
- where we lack courage
- what threatens us
- what renders us cruel
- how we remain limitlessly immature

At the end of it all, after an ideal ninety years of cogitation, we'll have done very well indeed if we have managed to secure just a few remotely reliable maps of one or two miniscule corners of the territory. We need to develop a compassionate, tender sense of humour for this curious bipedal creature who – alone among the animals – isn't only alive but is additionally condemned to wonder why they might be so. Socrates told us to know ourselves; he was careful to add a legendary, infinitely-hard-to-absorb addendum: that the beginning of wisdom is to know, at last, how little one knows.

Illustration list

Also available from The School of Life:

How to Understand Yourself

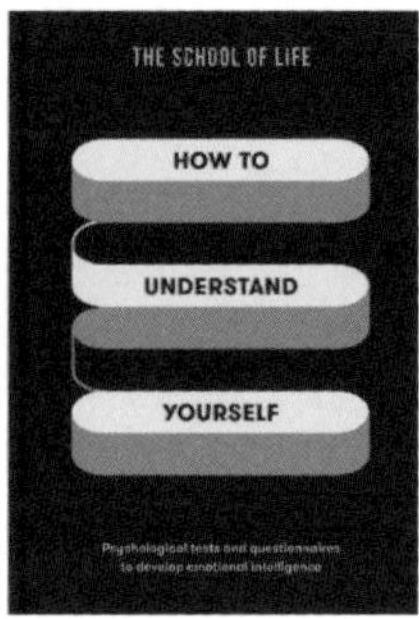

A book of psychological tests, questions and exercises – and how they can help you to know yourself better.

We spend our lives inside ourselves and yet understanding our inner world remains one of our most complex challenges. This enlightening and practical book offers a collection of transformative psychological tests designed to illuminate the hidden dimensions of our psyches.

Through a curated selection of fifty psychological exercises, you'll embark on an intimate journey of self-discovery. These tests invite you to look beneath the surface of your conscious thoughts, uncovering the subtle narratives that shape your emotions, relationships and sense of self.

Each test is an invitation to explore your unspoken fears, your deepest desires and the unconscious patterns that drive your behaviours, providing unprecedented insight into your inner workings.

ISBN: 978-1-916753-22-8

Also available from The School of Life:

Who Am I?

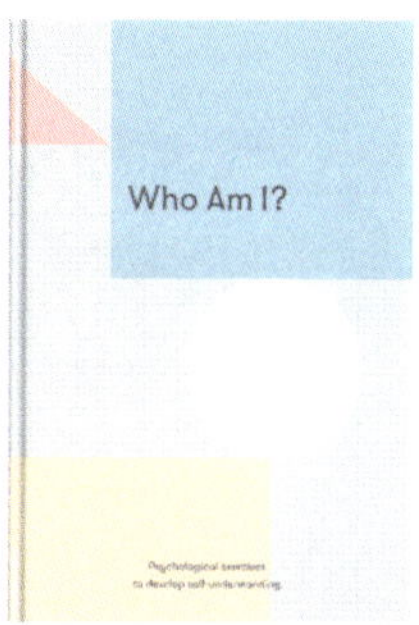

An interactive guide to our complex and elusive inner selves.

One of the trickiest tasks we ever face is that of working out who we really are. If we're asked directly to describe ourselves, our minds tend to go blank. We can't just sum ourselves up. We need prompts and suggestions and more detailed enquiries that help tease out and organise our picture of ourselves.

This book is designed to help us create a psychological portrait of who we are with the use of some unusual, oblique, entertaining and playful prompts. The book is filled with exercises to help us develop our self-understanding within key areas of our lives – helping to create a rich picture of our existence.

ISBN: 978-1-912891-08-5

Also available from The School of Life:

From Trauma to Healing

A guide to understanding our own trauma and finding ways to recover from it.

All of us have – to a greater or lesser extent – suffered from traumas in our lives, often at a young age. The less we address these traumas, the more they have a habit of causing us difficulties in the form of broken relationships, nagging anxieties, depression or physical symptoms like insomnia, digestive issues or back ache.

This book helps us understand what trauma is, how it can affect us and how we can liberate ourselves from its unfair and painful legacy. At once deeply practical and packed with ideas, the book functions like a humane and wise guide through a range of our most puzzling psychological difficulties. We are shown how to understand our pasts, assess our pains and finally say goodbye to troubles and repetitive patterns that have dogged us for too long.

This – at last – is a route to liberation and the calm self-awareness and fulfilment we have been searching for.

ISBN: 978-1-916753-19-8

Also available from The School of Life:

What They Forgot to Teach You at School

A collection of the essential emotional lessons we need in order to thrive.

We probably went to school for what felt like a very long time. We probably took care of our homework. Along the way, we surely learnt intriguing things about equations, the erosion of glaciers, the history of the Middle Ages and the tenses of foreign languages.

But why, despite all the lessons we sat through, were we never taught the really important things that dominate and trouble our lives: who to start a relationship with, how to trust people, how to understand one's psyche, how to move on from sorrow or betrayal and how to cope with anxiety and shame?

This book is a collection of our most essential lessons, delivered with directness and humanity, covering topics from love to career, childhood trauma to loneliness. To read this book is to be invited to lead kinder, richer and more authentic lives – and to complete an education we began but still badly need to finish. This is homework to help us make the most of the rest of our lives.

ISBN: 978-1-912891-39-9

Also available from The School of Life:

How Emotionally Mature Are You?

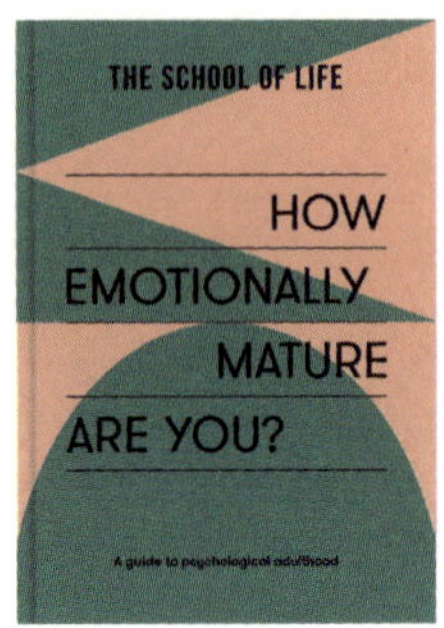

A roadmap for the emotionally mature adult.

Most of us long to be more emotionally mature and better able to face life's challenges with poise, confidence, kindness and good-natured intelligence. We want to be proper grown-ups. But to become so means, first and foremost, that we have to understand the many curious ways in which we might not currently be as mature as we would have hoped.

This is a questionnaire that helps us zero in on the key markers of psychological adulthood. We're prompted to look at how we typically respond to rejection, frustration, anxiety, ambiguity and hope. The book considers the influence of childhood, the role of self-love and the perils of perfectionism, as well as the best ways to achieve self-belief and overcome impostor syndrome. In a series of accompanying essays, we are given material to reflect on and shown how to reach the emotional age we aspire to be.

With candour, wisdom and rigour, the book delivers a realistic roadmap for how to grow into self-aware, un-frightened, joyful adults.

ISBN: 978-1-915087-12-6

Also available from The School of Life:

Self-Knowledge

A practical guide to knowing yourself.

In Ancient Greece, when the philosopher Socrates was asked to sum up what all philosophical commandments could be reduced to, he replied: 'Know Yourself'. Self-knowledge matters so much because it is only on the basis of an accurate sense of who we are that we can make reliable decisions – particularly around love and work.

This essay book takes us on a journey into our deepest, most elusive selves and arms us with a set of tools to understand our characters properly. We come away with a newly clarified sense of who we are, what we need to watch out for when making decisions and what our priorities and potential might be.

ISBN: 978-0-9957535-0-1

Also available from The School of Life:

A Voice of One's Own

A story about confidence and self-belief.

This is a novel with a striking mission at its heart: not just to tell us a story but to show us – through the example of one life – how we might change our own.

The novel introduces us to Anna, a kind, inspiring, thoughtful but modest and self-questioning person, in whom we might catch echoes of ourselves. Life has been hard of late for Anna: her job is putting her under extreme pressure, her relationship is lacking the support she craves, her parents have saddled her with a complicated emotional history. And yet she is determined to progress and liberate herself from her inhibitions.

In a style that's brief and poignant, accompanied by lyrical and thought-provoking images, we follow Anna as she slowly unpicks the roots of her self-suspicion and discovers something we all deserve but have so often been denied: a voice of our own.

ISBN: 978-1-916753-10-5

Also available from The School of Life:

Reasons to be Hopeful

What remains consoling, inspiring and beautiful.

In a world that isn't short of darkness, there can be few more urgent priorities than to spend time rehearsing for ourselves why life – despite all its challenges – still has so much to offer us; why there are still so many reasons to be hopeful.

Here is a collection of some of the most persuasive arguments for staying on the side of optimism, creativity, kindness, calm and hope. Across a series of essays, we learn why we still have the right to feel purposeful and buoyant despite everything that is challenging: because there is still so much more to discover, because love can triumph sometimes, because we are very small things in a mighty and beautiful universe and because we don't require perfection for things to feel good enough.

The book urges us to reconnect with our more resilient selves, bidding us to recover faith in what is still possible. At points funny and always encouraging and kind, here is an ideal friend to guide us back to courage and delight.

ISBN: 978-1-912891-89-4

To join The School of Life community and find out more,
scan below:

The School of Life publishes a range of books on essential topics in psychological and emotional life, including relationships, parenting, friendship, careers and fulfilment. The aim is always to help us to understand ourselves better and thereby to grow calmer, less confused and more purposeful. Discover our full range of titles, including books for children, here:

www.theschooloflife.com/books

The School of Life also offers a comprehensive therapy service, which complements and draws upon, our published works:

www.theschooloflife.com/therapy

THESCHOOLOFLIFE.COM